mountmellick embroidery

inspired by nature

Second edition published by Vetty Creations.
PO Box 1723, Hornsby Westfield NSW 1635, Australia
Copyright © Yvette Stanton and Prue Scott 2004, 2007.
Reprinted 2009, 2010, 2011.

www.vettycreations.com.au

First published in Australia in 2004 by Kangaroo Press,
an imprint of Simon & Schuster (Australia) Pty Ltd.

**The National Library of Australia
Cataloguing-in-Publication data**

Stanton, Yvette.
    Mountmellick embroidery: inspired by nature

    2nd ed.
    Bibliography.
    Includes index.
    ISBN 9780975767726 (pbk.).

    1. White work embroidery. 2. White work
    embroidery – Patterns. I. Scott, Prue. II. Title.

746.44042

Book design: Yvette Stanton, Vetty Creations
Printed in China

For Tim, Ben and Sophie – P. S.

For John, Emma and Iona – Y. S.

ACKNOWLEDGMENTS
The authors wish to thank all those who have helped
in the research and creation of this book.

Yvette would particularly like to thank:
John Stanton; Yvonne and Frank Wilkey; Joan Stanton;
Sister Teresa Margaret McCarthy; Sandra Counahan;
Dianne Lewandowski; Mary Dolan and the Mountmel-
lick Development Association; Valerie Wilson at the
Ulster Folk and Transport Museum; Alex Ward at the
National Museum of Ireland; Annie Kelly; The Mount-
mellick Embroidery Group; Dolores Dempsey at the
Mountmellick Museum, Mountmellick; Sarah Lalor;
Patricia Braga; Jo Mason; Abigail McEvoy; Helen Pers-
son and Charlotte Samuels at the Victoria & Albert
Museum; Julia Collingwood; Helen Golic; Megan John-
son; Janine Flew; Effie Mitrofanis; Dorothy Morgan,
Pam Breukhoven and Maria Xeros-Colbert at the
Embroiderers' Guild, Victoria; Gladys Giltrap; Melody
Lord; Jocelyn, Dianne and Louise at the Hornsby Wool
and Craft Nook.

Prue wishes to thank:
Tim Scott; Yvonne and Frank Wilkey; John Stanton;
John and Sheelagh Scott; Julia Collingwood; Helen
Golic; Megan Johnson; Janine Flew; Jocelyn, Dianne,
Louise and Sarah at the Hornsby Wool and Craft Nook;
Gladys Giltrap; Patricia Selkirk; Melody Lord.

mountmellick embroidery

inspired by nature

YVETTE STANTON & PRUE SCOTT

vetty creations

Contents

What is Mountmellick
  embroidery? 6
The history of Mountmellick
  embroidery 7
Examples of Mountmellick
  embroidery 10

Stitch instructions and
techniques 13

Materials, equipment and
  preparation for stitching.....14
  Fabric 14
  Thread 14
  Needles..............................15
  Hoop or frame 15
  Tracing the design 15
  Guide lines 15
  Linear and filling stitches 15
  Left-handed stitchers 15
  Starting and finishing stitching.15
Mountmellick stitches
  step-by-step........................16
Back stitch 16
  Seed stitch 16
Bokhara couching 16
Bullion stitch 17
  Double bullion 18
  Overwrapped bullion 18
Buttonhole fringe.........................18
  Buttonhole fringe – locked......18
  Buttonhole fringe – up and
    down....................................19
Buttonhole stitch 20
  Turning a sharp corner 20
  Simple buttonhole variations...20
  Detached buttonhole filling.....21
  Knotted buttonhole................22
  Whipped buttonhole..............22
Cable chain stitch 23

Starting a new thread 23
Cable chain, zigzagging 23
Cable plait stitch........................24
  Starting a new thread 24
  Turning a sharp corner 24
  Overcast cable plait 24
Chain stitch 25
  Starting a new thread 25
  Turning a sharp corner 25
  Reverse chain stitch 25
  Detached chain/lazy daisy
    stitch 26
Coral knot stitch.........................26
Cording stitch.............................26
Couching 27
Cretan stitch 27
Feather stitch 28
  Double feather stitch..............28
  Long-armed feather stitch 29
  Double long-armed feather
    stitch 29
  Buttonholed feather stitch.......29
  Single feather stitch 29
  Closed feather stitch...............30
  Upright feather stitch 30
Fly stitch.....................................30
French knot 31
Herringbone stitch......................31
Indian filling..............................32
Loop stitch.................................32
Mountmellick stitch....................33
  Alternating Mountmellick
    stitch 33
Palestrina knot 34
Running stitch 34
Satin stitch.................................34
  Filling shapes with distinct
    ends 35
  Padded satin stitch 35
Spider web 35

Stem stitch 36
   Outline stitch 36
   Turning a sharp corner 36
   Portuguese stem stitch 36
   Whipped stem stitch 37
Straight stitch.............................37
Thorn stitch...............................37
Trellis filling...............................38
Vandyke stitch 38
Waste knot.................................38
Wheat ear stitch 39
Whipped cord button 39

Knitting instructions and techniques 40
Materials and equipment 41
   Knitting needles 41
   Yarn.......................................41
   Left-handed knitters...............41
   Knitted fringe methods 41
**Knitting techniques
   step-by-step.......................42**
Making a slip knot.......................42
Casting on 42
Knitted fringe method 1 43
Knitted fringe method 2 44
Knitted fringe method 3 45
Casting off.................................46
Attaching the fringe 46

Projects with traditional applications..................47
Beginner projects
Leaf sampler...............................48
Blackberry doily..........................51
Honeysuckle doily 53
Shamrock and lily doily 55
Intermediate projects

Wheat mat.................................58
Morning glory brush and
   comb bag 60
Oval dogrose doily 63
Lily and forget-me-not
   nightdress case.....................66
Advanced projects
Blackberry table runner 71
Shamrock, thistle and rose
   tablecloth 76
Clematis and fern pillow sham.....80

Projects with contemporary applications....................85
Beginner projects
Oak leaf needlecase 86
Lily box 87
Framed flower spray picture.........90
Intermediate project
Grapes lampshade 91
Advanced projects
Wildflower table runner...............94
Passionflower and maidenhair
   fern bolster..........................98

Appendices 102
   Appendix 1 – Suppliers of
      Mountmellick materials 102
   Appendix 2 – Museum
      collections with Mountmellick
      embroidery..........................102
Bibliography and further reading.103
Index 103

Pattern sheets
Two double-sided pattern sheets are included with this book containing the patterns which are not found within its pages.

What is Mountmellick embroidery?

For those who have never encountered Mountmellick embroidery, it is often difficult to explain exactly what makes it distinct from other forms of embroidery, particularly crewel embroidery, which it most closely resembles. The following features are regarded as being characteristic of Mountmellick work.

WHITEWORK

Mountmellick is worked in white cotton thread on white cotton fabric. No colour is used.

COTTON SATIN JEAN

The fabric used for Mountmellick embroidery is heavy cotton satin jean, also known as cotton sateen. Due to the satin weave, the fabric has a low-level sheen.

MATT THREAD

Matt thread is used, as a contrast to the sheen of the fabric. Often only one or two different thicknesses of thread were used on each piece. When the work was very large, for example, a bedcover, the threads used were very thick, in keeping with the scale.

NATURE AS INSPIRATION

The subject matter is based on nature, and is usually floral. The flowers used were initially those found in the hedgerows of Mountmellick and along the banks of the River Owenass, which flows through the town. These include blackberry, dogrose, shamrock, fern and oak. There are some notable exceptions, such as the tiger lily and passionflower which, although they may have grown in Mountmellick, would have been found only in hothouses. As time progressed, more plants were added to designs, including cyclamen, narcissus, wheat, grapes and ivy. Occasionally shells, butterflies and naïve birds can be found on historical designs. Even less frequently, pineapples, vases and baskets have been known to appear.

BIG AND BOLD

The shapes are big and bold – Mountmellick designs are not small and dainty. While the stitching itself may be exquisite in its detail and quality, the motifs are large and expressive. The leaves and flowers are usually at least life-size, if not larger. Think big – not small!

EDGING

Mountmellick embroidery typically has a buttonholed edge, with a knitted fringe attached to it. The fringe is never cut, nor should it be crocheted or replaced with lace. Sometimes historical pieces do not have the knitted fringe, but just a buttonhole edging. Often the buttonhole (with or without fringe) is scalloped or curved. The buttonhole stitch may be one of a number of variations including padded, sawtooth or knotted.

HIGHLY TEXTURED

Mountmellick is a highly textured form of embroidery, with many knotted and padded stitches employed. Because no colour is used in Mountmellick embroidery, it is the texture of the stitches that brings much of the variation and interest.

Much use is made of padded satin stitch, bullions and large french knots. While some historical examples are quite two dimensional, Mountmellick embroidery is at its best when the stitching has a high degree of texture.

Mountmellick embroidery typically has no open work or eyelets. Although eyelets do appear on some historical articles, this is very rare and is not characteristic of the work. Mountmellick is certainly not lace as it is so often described!

APPLICATION

Mountmellick embroidery is very sturdy due to the heavy fabric and bold stitching. This meant that it was entirely suitable for everyday items of household use, and not just embroidery for special or best items. After use it could be boiled clean again, and its whiteness restored.

Traditionally the articles to which Mountmellick embroidery was applied included nightdress cases, brush and comb bags, bedspreads, pillow shams, table centres, runners and doilies.

The history of Mountmellick embroidery

The history of Mountmellick embroidery has unfolded in three distinct stages: its invention by Johanna Carter, a revival by Mrs Millner and a subsequent revival by Sister Teresa Margaret McCarthy. After the first two stages, Mountmellick embroidery declined in popularity and could have been forgotten, so we are very fortunate to have this style of embroidery today.

Mountmellick embroidery is named after the town in Ireland where it originated. In the late 1700s, Mountmellick, County Laois (pronounced 'Leash'), previously Queen's County, was very prosperous and was known as the 'Manchester of Ireland' for its successes in the milling, spinning and weaving of cotton.

Mrs Johanna Carter is credited with the invention of Mountmellick embroidery. It is often suggested that she was a member of the Religious Society of Friends (also known as the Quakers); however, an 1824 educational report describes her as a member of the Church of Ireland.

Around 1825, Johanna Carter was teaching embroidery to a group of fifteen local Mountmellick women and their daughters, seven of whom were Catholic and eight of whom were Protestant. Of the students taught by Johanna Carter, it is believed that the last died in approximately 1870.

It is likely that the embroidery Johanna Carter taught was based on the crewel style popular in Europe at the time and included some stitches that she had invented or adapted herself. White cotton thread and fabric were used due to their ready availability in Mountmellick. The designs were based on nature, and featured plants that grew locally in the wild, particularly along the banks of the local Owenass River.

In the household records of 1847 for Adare House in County Limerick, it is recorded that a bedspread was purchased from J. Carter (Johanna Carter). It is highly probable that this piece would have been made in Mrs Carter's new white-work style, and as such, this was most likely the first recorded sale of Mountmellick embroidery. The

The Owenass River flows through the town of Mountmellick in County Laois.

embroidery continued to be popular during the middle of the century, but as with many new fads, as time passed, interest in this new style of embroidery declined.

Ireland was a country dependent on agriculture and, in particular, the potato crop. Potatoes were the staple food of more than half the population. In 1845, the potato crop failed due to potato blight. Again in 1846 and 1847 the crops failed, each time more severely than before. The widespread famine that resulted from these successive failures meant that millions died from starvation and disease, when the rest of Europe's population was increasing. Many Irish emigrated in an effort to escape the dire situation. The famine brought poverty to everyone in Ireland except the very rich, who could still afford to pay the highly inflated prices for food. Following the failure of the first crop in 1847, the September crop was successful, but only a very small amount had been planted due to the shortage of seed. Thus began the very slow process of rebuilding. As the grip of the potato famine took hold across Ireland from 1846 onwards, the Religious Society of Friends was among the charities and religious groups who sought to aid needy people. Even as an industrial town, Mountmellick experienced great hardship as many became unemployed and had little money. In 1880, as the country was still rebuilding itself, Mrs Millner, a member of the Religious Society of Friends, started an industrial association to aid 'distressed Irish gentlewomen'. As a means of employment, the women produced embroidered articles in the style that Johanna Carter had previously developed. At the association's peak, around 1890, there were fifty workers producing embroidery for sale, but numbers declined as poverty decreased, and it had ceased production by the beginning of World War One.

O'Connell Square, formerly known as Drogheda Square, Mountmellick. The square features fine examples of Georgian architecture dating back to the 1700s.

Patrick Street (previously known as Henry Street) Mountmellick.

Quaker women continued to stitch and teach Mountmellick embroidery, the white on white style being consistent with their doctrines requiring plainness and simplicity. Along with other styles of embroidery, Mountmellick was taught as part of the curriculum to the girls at the Religious Society of Friends' School in Mountmellick.

From 1890 to 1898, during the time that Mrs Millner's organisation in Mountmellick was using the embroidery as a means to earn a living, Weldon Publishers in London produced a series of eight booklets on Mountmellick embroidery for the English market. These booklets introduced the style of embroidery to ladies who could afford the time to sit and stitch for pleasure (as had been the case in Johanna Carter's day). Similar publications were also available in America. Projects were also included in women's journals so that women could make their own pieces. These new projects published were more stylised than the natural style of former designs.

Articles of Mountmellick embroidery were purchased by travellers on their way to America, often at the port of Cobh, County Cork. In this way the popularity of the work spread further afield. It is somewhat surprising that although the embroidery is so sturdy in nature, to date there are not great numbers of examples that have surfaced in family linen collections.

In 1921, the Religious Society of Friends sold their school in Mountmellick to the Sisters of the Presentation Order. The nuns continued to run the school, teaching embroidery to the students as part of the curriculum. It is not known whether Mountmellick embroidery was taught; certainly as more of the school's teachers began to come from parts of Ireland where it was uncommon, there would have been fewer teachers who could instruct the girls in the Mountmellick style. In the records of the convent, there is no mention of Mountmellick embroidery until the 1970s.

Shortly before 1970, Sister Teresa Margaret McCarthy of the convent began to investigate the lost art of Mountmellick embroidery, having found one pattern within the convent. Sister Teresa experimented with the design, working it in colour, as one would for crewel embroidery. A request for information about and examples of the embroidery was sent throughout the town and its surroundings, and pieces were uncovered among family linen. From these, much was learnt about the embroidery, including the fact that it was always worked in white on white. Using her existing knowledge of embroidery, the scant information she could unearth and the few examples of Mountmellick work as reference, Sister Teresa taught herself the extra stitches that are unique to the Mountmellick style – and then began to teach others.

In 1970, the first piece of Mountmellick embroidery, a coverlet, was donated by the Scully family to the Presentation Convent, thus beginning their collection. In the 1970s, a local Quaker family by the name of Pim presented a trunk to the convent. Thinking it was just another trunk, it was put into storage and it was not until some time later that its bounty was discovered – the trunk was full of old Mountmellick embroidery patterns designed by members of the Pim family and their friends. It is also likely that some were bought (prices can be seen written on some patterns), and had been ordered from catalogues of embroidery patterns. For many years, the Pim trunk was taken to Sister Teresa's embroidery classes for the designs to be copied and adapted by the stitchers. More recently, copies have been made of all these designs, so that the precious originals can be preserved.

Mountmellick embroidery continues to flourish both in the town of Mountmellick and further afield. Classes in Mountmellick embroidery are taught throughout Ireland and around the world. As more people are educated about this traditional style of whitework embroidery, more will appreciate its great beauty and want to learn to stitch it for themselves.

The Religious Society of Friends' School in Mountmellick opened in 1786 initially only for girls, with boys admitted the following year. The school closed in 1920. From 1921 onwards it operated as St Mary's College, until it became the Mountmellick Community School in 1989.

9

Examples of Mountmellick embroidery

Detail of the border of the An Grianán quilt.

Detail of a leaf form from the An Grianán quilt. This scrolling leaf is worked in feather stitch and cable plait stitch.

By studying examples of Mountmellick embroidery, much can be learned about the designs and how stitches were used to interpret those designs. If you have the opportunity to view historical examples in museums, do so – so much can be learned by studying the real thing!

Some Mountmellick designs are filled with stitching, leaving very little unstitched ground. A beautiful example of this is the An Grianán quilt (from the collection of the An Grianán Adult Education Centre, Termonfechin, County Louth). There is a very wide border of embroidery around the edges, with a large centre section also completely filled. This design mixes scale, with large shapes in thick thread contrasting with small motifs in finer thread. Amongst the unusual subject matter are a pineapple, a basket and sunflowers. There are also a few small sections of detached buttonhole fillings, which are not a particularly common feature of Mountmellick embroidery.

The blackberry nightdress case, opposite, is an excellent example of a Mountmellick nightdress case. The knitted fringe is attached to sawtooth buttonhole in wavy scallop shapes. The fringe has five strands of yarn knitted together to make it very full. The motifs are blackberries, with a monogram positioned at the top of the front flap. The stitching is very well executed, with attractive choice of stitches.

When the leaves on the plant occur in groupings, such as the blackberries on the nightdress case, usually odd number groupings are used, for example, one, three or five. Within each group, all the leaves are worked similarly, but each grouping is different to the others.

Mountmellick embroidery typically has highly raised stitching due to the use of knotted and padded stitches. When looking at historical examples of Mountmellick, it is interesting to see that some stitchers used very two-dimensional stitching, while others used highly padded stitching. Occasionally stitchers actually couched over small wads of fabric with herringbone stitch and then worked satin stitch over the top for a very high relief effect.

Historically, Mountmellick stitchers were very innovative in their use of stitches. Many of the stitches are common ones that embroiderers familiar with styles such as crewel work would know. However, there are a number of stitches that are unique to Mountmellick embroidery. Among these are mountmellick stitch and thorn stitch, which is essentially a feather stitch with a french knot worked into it. Interestingly, neither of these stitches has been found on historical examples. Maybe this is because they were not popular with stitchers, or they were not developed until later. However, at some point they have become associated with Mountmellick embroidery, Mountmellick embroidery is perhaps one of the earliest styles of embroidery to use the bullion stitch.

The lily box top (page 87) illustrates the creative use of bullions in the flower petals, where they are substituted for some of the satin stitch. The blackberry table runner (page 71) shows how large french knots with many wraps are clustered tightly together to create wonderfully textural blackberries. The runner also uses cord buttons as blackberries. These are created by twisting lengths of thread to make a thick cord, and then whip stitching the cord to itself to build up a button. This technique was discovered on some historical examples of Mountmellick.

Stitches are often combined in an interesting way to create unusual effects. One such example is a variation on feather stitch with buttonhole stitch worked down the arms. The combination of the two stitches gives a fern-like quality. This technique is used in the framed flower spray picture (page 90). Other stitches are whipped, overcast or adapted to create new variations.

In pieces where the main design does not fill the whole surface, sometimes powdering (or sprigging) is used to fill the remaining space. Powdering is the use of small motifs, scattered randomly or in a pattern, to fill an otherwise empty space. On the clematis and fern pillow sham shown on page 80, the main design is on the ends, with regularly spaced double bullions (two together) filling the centre. On the shamrock and lily doily (page 55), the powdering takes the form of small padded satin-stitched shamrocks with bullions as the stalks. In this example, the main design is in the centre, with the powdering filling the spaces around the edges.

On large-scale items such as bedspreads, the motifs are often large in scale and stitched in thick thread. In these cases, the thread used is often the equivalent of 8 ply (UK: DK) knitting cotton.

Some designs use very few stitches. Sister Teresa tells of a 9 x 9-foot bedspread that used predominantly french knots and only a small amount of satin stitch. Indeed, some of the most striking examples use only a small number of stitches.

The edging of Mountmellick embroidery pieces varies greatly. The knitted fringe attached to buttonhole stitch is the traditional edging; however some pieces have only the buttonhole edging. It is unclear why this is the case, as the knitted fringe is charac-

Blackberry nightdress case. Nightdress cases were a popular application for Mountmellick embroidery.
Private collection.

11

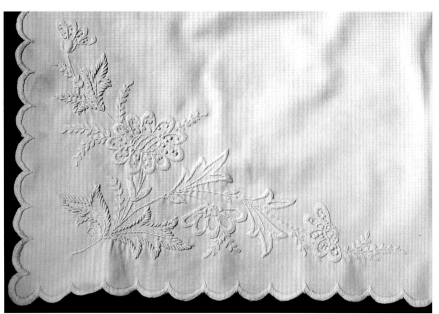

Daisy pillow sham (detail). This pillow sham has the same motif repeated and reflected in each corner, with different stitch interpretation each time. The edge is finished with a scalloped buttonhole. There is no knitted fringe attached.

Private collection.

teristic of Mountmellick embroidery. It could be that the creator did not have enough thread to knit a fringe (perhaps due to cost), maybe they couldn't knit, or perhaps the piece originally had a fringe that has since been removed.

Some Mountmellick embroidery has a sewn fringed buttonhole edging though this is not seen on many museum pieces (see oval dogrose doily, page 63). There are examples in museums that have different edgings, such as crochet or lace, which are not historically accurate representations of the technique. In the collection of the Victoria & Albert Museum, London, there is a lace-edged nightdress case which is the example of Mountmellick work commonly shown in embroidery books. Such edgings are not typical.

The knitted fringe varies in width from piece to piece, from the very wide fringe – approximately 10cm (4in) long loops, which can look extremely straggly and messy – to the more common narrower fringe, approximately 5cm (2in) in width. The 'lace' section of the fringe usually has one to two ridges of thick knitting, with open lacy sections in between. Depending on which knitting pattern is used, the first ridge may be sewn directly to the buttonhole, or may have an edge of loops which means it sits a little way out from the buttonhole edge.

The fringe is never cut. To make a very full fringe, three or four of the threads used for the embroidery are knitted as one. The complete length that is required is knitted, most of the stitches are cast off, and then the remaining two or three stitches are unravelled completely down one side of the knitting. It is this unravelling that creates the fringe, whilst allowing the rest of the knitting to remain intact. The knitted fringe is then neatly sewn onto the buttonhole edging.

The buttonhole edge to which the fringe is attached can differ greatly from example to example. Many variations of buttonhole stitch are used, such as plain, padded, knotted and sawtooth. The buttonhole can have straight sides, with square or curved corners, or repeating concave or convex scallops.

Traditionally, patterns are supplied as line drawings only with no indication of which stitches to use. It is up to the individual stitcher to interpret the design and to decide what stitch to use where. In this book, each of the projects has the stitches fully specified, but readers are welcome to experiment with their own interpretations of the designs.

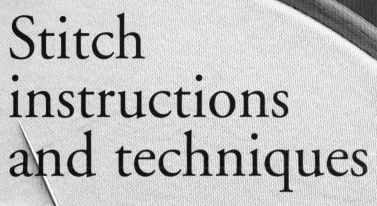

Stitch instructions and techniques

Mountmellick embroidery typically has highly raised stitching due to the use of many knotted and padded stitches. Historically, Mountmellick embroiderers were very innovative in their use of stitches.

There are many stitches in Mountmellick embroidery that are common to other embroidery styles. However, in Mountmellick embroidery they are combined in interesting ways to create unusual effects.

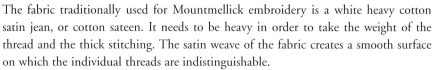

Materials, equipment and preparation

Finding authentic threads and fabrics can be problematic as they can be very difficult to source. Specialist suppliers carry fabric and threads specifically for Mountmellick embroidery. See suppliers listing (Appendix 1, page 102).

In selecting your materials, be aware that by not using authentic threads and fabric, you will be departing from the traditional style of Mountmellick embroidery. When learning a new style of embroidery one should try to use the traditional threads and fabrics to get the right effect.

FABRIC

The fabric traditionally used for Mountmellick embroidery is a white heavy cotton satin jean, or cotton sateen. It needs to be heavy in order to take the weight of the thread and the thick stitching. The satin weave of the fabric creates a smooth surface on which the individual threads are indistinguishable.

Zweigart produce a white cotton satin fabric called Satin Royal (product code 3211). This fabric is very suitable for Mountmellick embroidery. While not carried as regular stock in most countries, it can be special-ordered from needlework shops. Whilst this is one of the best options, there are other alternatives. Always use high-quality fabrics, so that your work will look its best. A low-quality fabric or one that is not heavy enough may spoil your piece when washed.

Zweigart Satin Royal fabric has a very fine satin weave.

Washing

Traditional fabric is cream and must be boiled to become white. If using an alternative fabric, use one that is already white. Fabrics should be washed before use to remove the size in the fabric and to allow the fabric to shrink as needed.

To boil the fabric white

When fabrics need to be whitened, at the completion of stitching and before attaching the fringe, soak the finished piece for several hours in cold water. Place the embroidery in a large pot of water with soap flakes. Bring the water to the boil for a few minutes, then discard the water. Refill the pot with cold water – no extra soap – and boil again. Repeat until all the soap suds have gone (three to five times), and the embroidery is whitened.

Dry the washed piece flat in the shade. To iron, place the work face down on a well-padded surface, such as clean thick towels. Steam iron gently from the back to remove any creases without flattening the stitching.

THREAD

Traditional Mountmellick threads had no shine. For this reason mercerised cottons or perle cottons are not suitable for Mountmellick embroidery.

Differing weights of thread were used, though usually only two at the most within the one piece. Larger items such as bedspreads were often worked in thick cotton – about 8 ply (UK: DK) knitting cotton – due to the scale of both the piece and the design. Smaller articles such as doilies or pillow shams used finer cotton, more akin to 4 ply knitting cotton. There were occasionally sections of detached buttonhole used as a filler, in very fine cotton.

Mountmellick threads are very different to work with compared to other embroidery threads. They are a soft, twisted, non-divisible cotton with a number of strands. Care needs to be taken when using them as they can easily untwist. It is important to keep the thread twisted as this will give much better results. If you notice that the thread is untwisting, retwist the thread back to its original state.

Mountmellick thread is a soft, finely twisted thread.

For those who choose not to use authentic-style threads, there are less suitable alternatives, such as cotton floche, coton à broder, soft cotton, candlewicking cotton and Presencia Super Finca. These will not produce an authentic Mountmellick effect, as each of these has its own particular disadvantages, for example, too much shine, not enough twist, or too fine. Knitting or crochet cotton is a more suitable alternative, though limited in its range of weights. Do not use a thread or yarn that is mercerised.

NEEDLES

The needles used for most stitching in Mountmellick embroidery are chenille needles, which have a sharp point, large eye and comparatively thick shaft. For whipped stitches where the needle does not need to go through the fabric, tapestry needles can be useful.

For knotted stitches in other styles of embroidery, straw needles or milliner's needles are used. However, Mountmellick threads are too thick to fit through the eye of these needles, so large darners should be used instead. To make very thick bullions and large french knots, very large darners can be used to increase the size of the wraps.

HOOP OR FRAME

You will need to use a hoop or frame when stitching Mountmellick embroidery. Without one, the heavy stitching will make the fabric pucker. Mount the fabric in the hoop or on the frame so that it is drum tight.

If using a hoop, remove the work from it at the end of each stitching session. Roll the work in a clean cloth to stop stubborn creases from forming and help to keep the work clean.

TRACING THE DESIGN

Photocopy the pattern at the size indicated. Position the fabric over the photocopy and trace using a sharpened HB pencil. Taping the fabric and pattern to a window or using a lightbox may help with visibility. After the completion of stitching, make sure all lines are removed. Many people do not recommend using water-soluble fabric markers, however if you choose to use one, follow the manufacturer's instructions at all times.

GUIDE LINES

The stitch instructions show the stitches worked on guide lines, to assist with understanding the stitch construction. They need not be used on the work. However, if using them, make sure they can be completely removed (e.g. washed out) or fully covered.

LINEAR AND FILLING STITCHES

Linear stitches are those that are used in lines, such as for outlines or stems. Filling stitches are those that are used to fill spaces, such as petals or leaves. Some stitches, depending on how they are used, can be both linear and filling stitches.

LEFT-HANDED STITCHERS

This book can be successfully used by left-handed embroiderers, however, the stitch instructions will need to be reversed. The easiest way is to substitute 'right' for 'left' and vice versa. Alternatively, everything can be rotated 90 degrees for comfortable insertion of the needle.

If reversing, it may also help to reverse the diagrams. This can be done by holding the page up to a light source and looking at the diagram from the back of the page, or with the acetate method: photocopy the diagrams onto photocopier acetate and flip it over to see the diagrams in reverse. You can also use a mirror to reverse the diagrams.

STARTING AND FINISHING STITCHING

To start stitching, run the needle under nearby stitching, on the back of the fabric. Take a small back stitch to secure the thread. If there is no nearby stitching, use a waste knot. To finish, run the needle under the stitching, on the back of the fabric. Trim the thread.

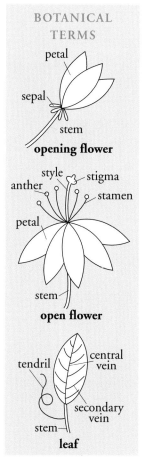

L–R, Chenille 22 needle, Darner 1 needle, Darner 14 needle, Tapestry 24 needle.

BOTANICAL TERMS

petal

sepal

stem

opening flower

style · stigma

anther · stamen

petal

stem

open flower

tendril

central vein

secondary vein

stem

leaf

To complete the projects, an understanding of the parts of plants and flowers is required.

Mountmellick stitches step-by-step

Back stitch

Back stitch is worked from right to left.

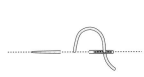  

1 Use one line. Bring the thread out on the line. Insert the needle back a short distance to the right. Bring the needle out again the same distance to the left of where the thread emerges.

2 Pull the needle and thread through.

3 To work subsequent stitches, insert the needle at the end of the previous stitch (in the same hole). Bring the needle out again the same distance to the left of the thread.

4 Repeat to build up a line of stitching. To finish, insert the needle back at the end of the previous stitch.

SEED STITCH

Seed stitch, or seeding, is a filling stitch made up of small randomly scattered back stitches.

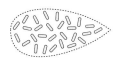  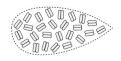 

1 Fill the shape with small, randomly scattered, individual back stitches. The stitches should be short – less than 2 mm (¹/₁₂ in) in length.

❶ *Shapes filled with seeding are usually outlined with another stitch on completion.*

❶ *Double seed stitch is where each stitch is worked twice to create thicker 'seeds'.*

Bokhara couching

Bokhara couching is a self-couched stitch – the laid thread is also used for the couching.

  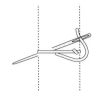 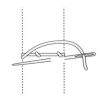

1 Use two guide lines. Bring the thread out of the left line and insert the needle into the right. Bring the needle and thread out a short distance along where the laid thread will lie.

2 Take a small diagonal stitch over the laid thread. Bring the needle out further along the laid thread.

3 Take a short diagonal stitch over the laid thread and bring the needle out again on the left line.
❶ *If the length of the laid stitches is longer than those shown here, use more couching stitches as needed.*

4 Insert the needle into the right guide, and bring the needle and thread out so that the tying down stitch will be evenly spaced between the two of the previous line.

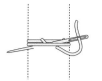

5 Continue to work evenly spaced couching stitches along the laid thread.

6 Repeat the process to build up a pattern of couched threads tying down the laid stitches.

❶ *The couching stitches should be short on the fabric front, and long on the back.*

❶ *The couching stitches can also be worked so that they line up with each other.*

❶ *By working the couching stitches so that they cross the laid stitch in the opposite direction, depending on the direction of twist of the thread, the couched stitch will either 'disappear' into the laid stitch, or become more pronounced. Either way can be used, producing different effects.*

Bullion stitch

Bullion stitch, which is often known as 'worms' to Mountmellick embroiderers, is a thick wrapped stitch. It can be used as a linear stitch, or as a filling stitch by working a number of adjacent stitches.

❶ *Use a straw (or milliner's) needle, as the shaft thickness does not increase at the eye, which makes it easier to pull the needle and thread through the wraps. Very thick cotton will not fit through the eye of a straw needle, so in this case use large darners.*

❶ *Thread the needle so that the thread tail is short. There will be less doubled thread to pull through the wraps.*

❶ *You will need to use a hoop or frame for this stitch.*

1 Mark the length of the bullion on the fabric. Bring the thread out at one end and insert the needle again at the other end.

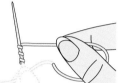

2 Bring the needle point out at the first end. Pull the needle part way through, so that most of it is above the fabric surface. Hold the eye of the needle below the fabric with your left hand. Wrap the thread around the needle three times in a clockwise direction.

3 Push the wraps down to the base of the needle to sit stacked against the fabric.

4 Wrap the thread clockwise around the needle a few more times.

5 Push the wraps down again to stack them. Repeat steps 4 and 5 as many times as necessary for the desired number of wraps.

❶ *By gently stroking the threads in a clockwise direction the wraps will become tighter. Conversely, stroking in an anticlockwise direction will produce looser wraps, which can be useful when struggling to pull the needle through.*

6 Loosely hold the wraps between your right thumb and forefinger. Gently pull the needle and thread through with your left hand.

7 Continue to gently pull the thread through the wraps until they lie flat against the fabric.

8 Insert the needle into the fabric at the end of the bullion.

9 Pull the thread through to the back to complete the bullion.

❶ *Wrapping in the opposite direction will create different results, because of the way the thread twists.*

❶ *Very long bullions can be couched in order to hold the full length in place.*

Double bullions are where two bullions are worked side by side.

Overwrapping makes curved bullions that sit up from the fabric surface or that can be couched to lay flat against it in their curved shape.

Create more wraps than are needed for the distance. Pull the needle through, and allow the bullion to sit up from the fabric rather than overtightening it to force the bullion to sit flat.

Buttonhole fringe

This is the simplest of three buttonhole fringes. Historically, the fringe length is usually about 1cm (³⁄₈in).

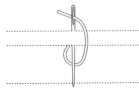 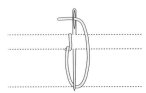 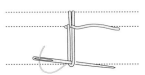 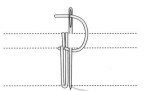

1 Bring the thread out on the middle line. A little to the right, insert the needle at the top and bring it out over the thread, on the middle line. Pull the needle through.

2 Next to the first stitch, insert the needle in at the top line and bring it out on the middle, over the thread. Leave the thread looped down to the bottom line to create the fringe.

❶ *To keep the fringe length uniform, thread another needle with some pale machine sewing thread. On the bottom guide line, tack each loop down through the fabric.*

3 Insert the needle in the top line. Bring the needle out over the thread, at the middle line. Pull the needle through to tighten the stitch.

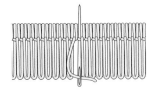 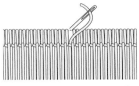 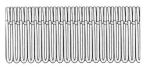 

4 Repeat steps 2 and 3 to build up a line of fringing. When the stitching meets the beginning, slip the last stitch into the first.

5 To finish, take the thread to the back through the top line.

6 Remove the tacking at the base of the loops when stitching is complete.

BUTTONHOLE FRINGE – LOCKED

This version of the buttonhole fringe is more stable than the first as it locks each fringe loop in place. Again use three guide lines, as for the simple buttonhole fringe.

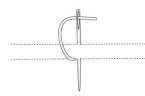 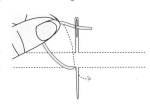 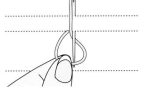 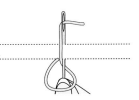

1 Bring the thread out on the middle line. Slightly to the right, insert the needle in the top line and out through the middle line.

2 Hold the thread near where it goes through the needle eye. Bring this part down and take it under the needle tip from left to right.

❶ *A loop will be formed around the needle point.*

3 Pull the needle down through the loop, and gently tighten so that the stitch is locked in place.

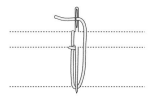

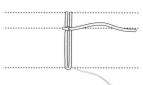

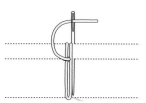

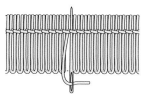

4 Insert the needle in the top line. Bring it out on the middle line. With the thread looped down to the bottom line, pull the needle through.

❶ *To keep the fringe length uniform, thread a needle with some pale machine sewing thread. On the bottom guide line, tack each loop down through the fabric.*

5 Slightly to the right, insert the needle at the top line and out through the middle line.

6 Repeat steps 2 through 5 to build up a line of fringing. Because this stitch is usually worked right around the edge of a shape, slip the last stitch into the first.

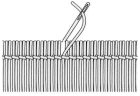

Pomegranates are a favourite motif

7 To finish, take the thread through to the back on the top line.

8 Remove the tacking when stitching is complete.

BUTTONHOLE FRINGE – UP AND DOWN

This fringe is based on the up and down buttonhole. Use three guide lines.

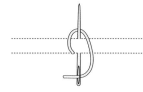

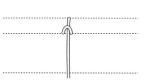

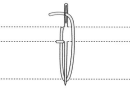

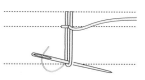

1 Bring the thread out on the middle line. A little to the right, insert the needle in the middle line and bring it out on the top line. Take the thread up behind the needle point.

2 Pull the needle through and then downwards to gently tighten the stitch.

3 Insert the needle in the top line and bring it out on the middle line. Leave the thread looped down to the bottom line. Take the needle point over the thread. Pull the needle through.

❶ *To keep the fringe length uniform, thread another needle with some pale machine sewing thread. On the bottom guide line, tack each loop down through the fabric.*

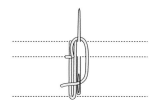

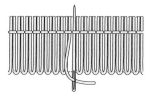

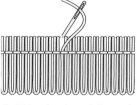

4 A little to the right, insert the needle in the middle line and bring it out on the top line. Take the thread up behind the needle point. Pull the needle through.

5 Continue repeating steps 2 to 4 until the stitching meets the beginning again. Slip the needle under the first stitch.

6 Take the thread through to the back on the top line.

7 Remove the tacking along the bottom line.

Buttonhole stitch

Buttonhole stitch is used to edge most articles of Mountmellick embroidery.
It is also used as a feature stitch in the embroidery.
When worked with the stitches spaced, this stitch is more correctly referred to as blanket stitch.

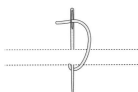 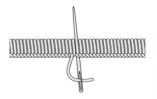 

1 Use two guide lines. Bring the thread out on the lower line. To the right, insert the needle from the top to the bottom line, with the needle point over the thread.

2 Insert the needle in the top line, and bring it out on the bottom line adjacent to the previous stitch. Pull the needle and thread through.

3 To join the end of the stitching up with the beginning (if working around an entire shape), slip the needle under the beginning of the first stitch.

4 Take the needle through to the back on the top line.
❶ *If the stitching does not need to go around an entire shape, to finish take a small stitch over the final stitch.*

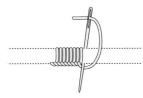 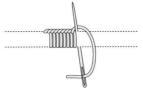

❶ *Sometimes the stitches appear to be on an angle, as if they are falling over. To counteract this, insert the needle at a slight angle rather than straight up and down.*

❶ *If it is more comfortable working away from yourself, the stitching can be rotated 180 degrees and worked with the rolled section at the top rather than the bottom.*

TURNING A SHARP CORNER

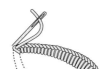 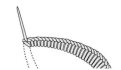

To turn a sharp corner, bring the needle out in the buttonhole at the corner point. Take a small stitch over the corner, to anchor the corner stitch.

Bring the needle out again in the corner buttonhole and continue stitching.

SIMPLE BUTTONHOLE VARIATIONS

Buttonhole variations can be created by padding, changing the length of the stitches used or curving the line of stitches.

Padded buttonhole	Stepped buttonhole	Sawtooth buttonhole 1	Sawtooth buttonhole 2

  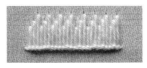 

Padded buttonhole is similar to padded satin stitch (see page 35), except that buttonhole stitch is worked over the padding, rather than satin stitch.

Use three guide lines. Stitch two shorter stitches, then two longer stitches.

Use four guide lines. Work stitches in groups of threes, with the first one longest, then each one successively shorter.

Use four guide lines. Work a short, then a medium, then a long length stitch. Work a medium, then a short. Continue, stepping up and down.

Wavy edged buttonhole	Concave scalloped edge	Convex scalloped edge	Wavy buttonhole edge

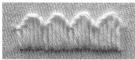  

Use four guide lines. Work it similarly to Sawtooth 2, instead lengthening and shortening the stitches at the rolled edge.

Angle the stitches to fit the curves and points.

Angle the stitches to fit the curves and points.

Angle the stitches to fit the curves.

DETACHED BUTTONHOLE FILLING

Detached buttonhole filling is used to fill shapes and motifs. Work the filling before any outlines. It is only attached to the fabric at the edges of the shape, and does not catch in any fabric elsewhere.

  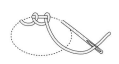 

1 Take a straight stitch across the top of the shape.

2 Bring the thread out on the edge of the shape, a short distance down. Take a buttonhole stitch through the straight stitch.
❶ *Keep the thread loosely looped. Aim to maintain a constant tension throughout.*

3 Spacing the stitches out, work buttonhole stitches through the straight stitch, to fill the width of the shape. Insert the needle and thread at the other edge.

4 Bring the needle and thread out on the guide line, a short distance below where the previous row ended. Take a buttonhole stitch through the bottom of the closest loop in the row above.

5 Continue across the row, working a buttonhole stitch into each loop from the previous row.

6 Repeat steps 4 and 5 back and forth to fill the shape. Finish with a stitch over the loop at the lower edge.

❶ *This stitch is normally outlined with another stitch on completion.*

Tiger lilies are very attractive motifs

21

A small knot at the end of each stitch creates texture. The stitches further apart than for regular buttonhole.

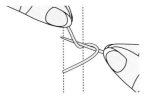 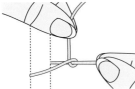 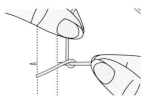 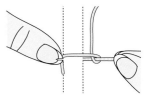

1 Using two guide lines, bring the thread out on the left line. Take the thread up over the front of the needle and around it once.

2 Without allowing the thread to slip off the point of the needle, insert the needle point in the right line, up a little from where the thread came out on the left.

3 Bring the needle out on the left line.

4 Lift the thread coming from the fabric up and tuck it behind the needle point.

❶ *Do not pull the needle all the way through yet.*

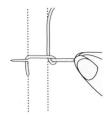  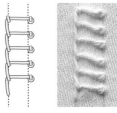 

Daisies feature on the antique pillow sham shown on page 12.

5 Tighten the thread around the needle.

6 Pull the needle and thread through to complete the first knotted buttonhole stitch.

7 Repeat the sequence to build up a line of stitching. To finish, take a small stitch over the final buttonhole.

WHIPPED BUTTONHOLE

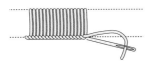 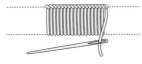 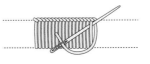

1 Work regular buttonhole using a long stitch length. Finish with a small stitch over the last buttonhole stitch.

2 Turn the work 180 degrees. Change to a tapestry needle. Bring the thread out at the other end of the stitching.

❶ *A tapestry needle slides more easily under the stitches.*

3 Slide the needle under the first stitch from left to right without entering the fabric. Ensure the needle goes above the thread.

4 Gently pull the thread up towards the looped section of the buttonhole to lock the stitch in place.

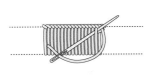 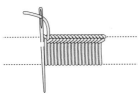  

5 Without entering the fabric, take the needle under the next buttonhole stitch. Gently pull the thread upwards to lock the stitch in place.

6 Whip all the buttonhole stitches. To finish the row, take a small stitch into the fabric, exiting just below the level of the previous row, ready to start the next.

7 Work back and forth along the rows to fill the desired section of buttonhole with whipping.

❶ *When worked on a buttonhole wheel, the whipping can be used in one direction as shown here, or alternate rounds can change direction as for the straight version.*

Cable chain stitch

Cable chain stitch is a close relation to cable plait stitch, and uses a similar technique.

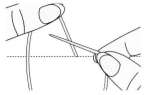 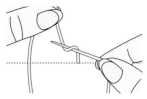 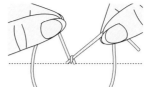 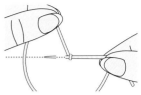

1 Use one guide. Bring the thread out on the line, and pull it upwards. Place the needle in front of the thread.

2 Wind the thread over the front of the needle and up behind it.

3 Insert the needle into the line a little way along from where it emerged.

4 Bring the needle out a little further along the line (using the desired stitch length).

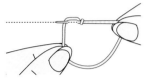 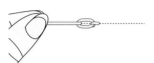  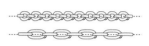

5 Take the thread down behind the needle.
❶ *Make sure the thread sits snugly around the needle.*

6 Pull the needle and thread through to gently tighten the chain and link.

7 Repeat steps 1 to 6 to build up a line of stitches. To finish, take a small stitch over the end of the last chain.

❶ *By varying the length of the chains or links, the effect can be changed to create a different look.*

STARTING A NEW THREAD

1 Finish the thread with a small stitch over the last chain. Fasten the thread in the back of the stitching.

2 Fasten the new thread at the back. Bring it out in the last chain. Continue stitching as before.

CABLE CHAIN, ZIGZAGGING

This is a variation of cable chain, where each chain is stepped up or down from the previous one.

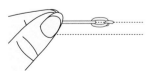 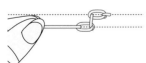  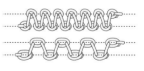

1 Use two guide lines. Work a single cable chain stitch on the top line.

2 Step down to the lower line and work another single cable chain stitch.

3 Work subsequent chains on alternate lines to build up a row of stitches. To finish, take a small stitch over the end of the last chain.

❶ *By varying the length of the chains or links, the effect can be changed to create a different look.*

Cable plait stitch

Cable plait stitch is also known as 'braid stitch' or 'figure of eight'. Practise will be required to master this stitch.

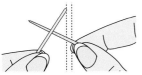

1 Use two guides, about 2mm (¹⁄₁₂in) apart. Bring the thread out on the left line. Lay it over the needle.
❶ *If the stitch is worked too wide it will be unstable.*

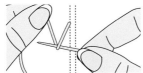

2 Take the thread up behind the needle.

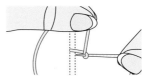

3 Hold the thread above the needle, and move the needle up and right, making sure the loop remains on the needle.

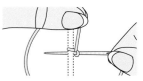

4 Slightly below where the thread emerges from the left line, enter the needle in the right line and bring it out on the left line.

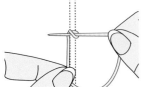

5 Take the thread down behind the needle point. Gently tighten so the knot fit snugly around the needle.
❶ *If you do not tighten the stitch at this point, the plait will be messy and misshapen.*

6 Pull the needle and thread through to gently tighten the stitch.
❶ *When tightening, pull to the left only, as this will allow the stitch to tighten whilst maintaining its shape.*

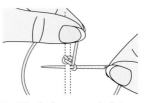

7 Work the next stitch just below the previous one.
❶ *Don't work the cable plaits too close together or they will look squashed and messy.*

8 Continue, building up a line of stitches. To finish, take a small stitch over the bottom of the final plait.
❶ *The finished stitch should be able to be flicked with a fingernail and not move.*

STARTING A NEW THREAD

1 To finish a thread, take a small stitch over the last cable plait. Fasten the thread through the back of the stitching.

2 Fasten the new thread in the back of the stitching. Bring the needle out in the previous stitch. Continue stitching as before.

TURNING A SHARP CORNER

1 To turn a sharp corner, stitch up to the corner and take a small stitch over the end to finish off.

2 Start the new line of stitching butted up against the previous one. Continue stitching as before.

OVERCAST CABLE PLAIT

1 Work a line of cable plait stitch. Bring the thread out on the third guide line, next to the first plait, and insert the needle into that plait. Pull the needle through to the back.

2 Bring the needle out on the line adjacent to the next plait and make another short stitch into the plait.

3 Continue in the same way until all the cable plait stitches have been overcast.
❶ *The length of the overcast stitch can be short or long, depending on the effect desired.*

❶ *Both sides of the cable plait stitch can be overcast, by working along one side, and then the other.*

Chain stitch

Chain stitch is usually a linear stitch, but can also be used as a filling or for padding under other stitches.

1 Use one guide line. Bring the thread out on the line. Insert the needle at the same point and bring it out again further along the line. Loop the thread underneath the needle point.

2 Pull the needle and thread through. Insert the needle into the first chain, on the line where the thread emerges. Bring the needle point back out again further along the line and take the thread under it.

3 Repeat to build up a line of chain stitches. To finish, anchor the final chain by taking a small stitch over its end.

Honeysuckle flowers are featured on the doily on page 53

STARTING A NEW THREAD

TURNING A SHARP CORNER

1 To finish a thread, take a small stitch over the last chain. Fasten the thread at the back of the stitching.

2 Fasten the new thread. Bring the needle out in the previous stitch. Continue stitching.

1 To turn a sharp corner, stitch up to the corner and take a small stitch over the end to finish off. Bring the needle out in the last chain.

2 Insert the needle in the chain, loop the thread under the needle point, and continue stitching.

REVERSE CHAIN STITCH

This stitch is worked in reverse compared to regular chain stitch. The final stitch is worked first and the remaining stitches are worked in behind it. This method can make stitch placement more precise as the needle position is more easily seen.

 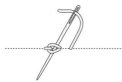  

1 Use one guide line. At the far end of the line, work one chain stitch (as explained above) with the anchoring stitch at the furthermost point.
❶ *Reverse chain stitch is worked from left to right.*

2 Bring the thread out on the line one stitch length back towards the beginning (unworked end). Without entering the fabric, take the needle under the two 'arms' of the previous chain.

3 Enter the needle next to where the thread emerges from the fabric thus completing the next chain.

4 Repeat steps 2 and 3 to build up a line of chain stitches, working back towards the beginning of the line.
❶ *As it is easier to see the whole stitch length while you work, reverse chain stitch can be useful for creating very regular chain stitching.*

Detached chain stitches are single chains. They can be used singly, in groups as flowers, or worked side by side as a filling stitch.

1 Bring the thread out of the fabric. Insert the needle into the same hole and bring it out a short distance away. Loop the thread under the needle point.

2 Pull the needle and thread through. Take a small stitch over the end to finish.

❶ *To work as a filling stitch, lengthen the chains and work subsequent stitches next to the first one. Detached chain as a filling can be stitched with or without padding.*

❶ *To work a lazy daisy flower, work the first chain angled towards 12 o'clock. Work the next ones at 5 and 7 o'clock. Work the final two at 10 and 2 o'clock.*

Coral knot stitch

Also known as 'snail trail', this stitch can be worked with the knots very closely spaced, or spread further apart.

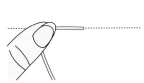 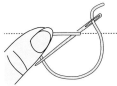 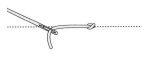 

1 Use one guide line. Bring the thread out on the guide line and hold it along the guide line and against the fabric with your thumb.

2 Take a tiny diagonal stitch through the fabric underneath the thread which is lying along the line. Bring the needle point out over the section of thread which loops up to the needle.

3 Pull the needle and thread through and tighten to create a small knot.

4 Repeat the steps to build up a line of knots. To finish, take a small stitch at the end of the final knot.

❶ *Varying the spacing of the knots will create different effects, as shown here.*

Cording stitch

This stitch is like a very compact slanting buttonhole or single feather. It should look like a thin, twisted cord.

  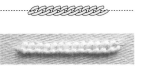

1 Use one guide line. Bring the thread out on the line. Diagonally insert the needle a small distance to the left, above the line. Bring the needle point out just below the line. Take the thread under the needle point.

❶ *Keep the stitch length very short and the spacing narrow, so that it looks like a finely twisted cord.*

2 Pull the needle and thread through. Diagonally insert the needle point above the line as close as possible to the previous stitch. Bring the needle out again just below the line. Take the thread under the needle point.

3 Continue in the same way to build up a line of stitches. To finish, take a small stitch over the final cord stitch.

Couching

Couching can be used as an outline or filling stitch. Any number of threads can be couched.

1 Use one guide line. Bring the threads to be couched (the laid threads) out on the guide line. Lay them flat along the line.

2 Hold the laid threads in place. Bring a new couching thread out below the laid threads near where they emerge. Take a small stitch over the laid threads, and bring the needle back out of the fabric at the position of the next stitch.

3 Repeat to build up a line of couching.

❶ *The laid threads should not pucker or be too loose, but should lie flat against the fabric.*

4 When the line of couching is complete, thread the laid threads into a needle and take them to the back of the fabric and secure.

The completed couching.

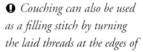

❶ *Couching can also be used as a filling stitch by turning the laid threads at the edges of*

the shape and couching them next to the previous line.

Cretan stitch

Cretan stitch is closely related to feather stitch. By varying stitch length and spacing different effects are obtained.

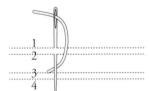

1 Work with four guides, numbered 1 to 4 from top to bottom. Bring the thread out on line 3. Slightly to the right, insert the needle in line 1 and bring it out again on line 2. Take the needle point over the stitch, and pull the needle and thread through.

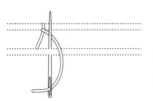

2 Slightly to the right, insert the needle in line 4 and bring it out again through line 3. Take the needle point over the thread, and pull the needle and thread through.

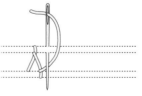

3 Slightly to the right, insert the needle in line 1, bringing it out again on line 2. Take the needle point over the thread, and pull the needle and thread through.

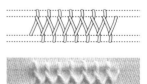

4 Continue, repeating steps 2 and 3 to build up a line of stitching. To finish, take the thread to the back on line 2 for an up stitch (as shown) or line 3 for a down stitch.

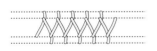

❶ *To work very open cretan stitch, space the stitches further apart.*

❶ *For closed cretan stitch, work the stitches very close together.*

Feather stitch

Feather stitch is a very versatile stitch with many variations. It is closely related to buttonhole and cretan stitch.

1 Use four guides, numbered 1 to 4, left to right. Bring the thread out on line 3. Level with this, insert the needle into line 1. Bring the needle out on line 2, a short way below. Pull the needle through.

2 Insert the needle into line 4, level with where the thread exits on line 2. Bring the needle out on line 3 using the previous stitch length. Pull the needle through.

3 Insert the needle into line 1 level with where the thread exits on line 3. Bring the needle and thread out on line 2 using the previous stitch length. Pull the needle through.

4 Repeat steps 2 and 3 to build up a line of stitching. To finish, take a small straight stitch over the final feather stitch.

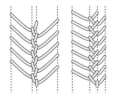

❶ *Altering the guide spacing and stitch length creates different effects.*

❶ *Feather stitch can also be worked away from you if preferred.*

Dogrose leaves provide wonderful motifs just ripe for stitch experimentation

DOUBLE FEATHER STITCH

Double feather stitch has two steps in each direction.

1 Use five guides, numbered 1 to 5, from left to right.

2 Bring the thread out on line 4. Level with this, insert the needle in line 2 . Bring the needle out on line 3, a short distance below. Pull the needle through.

3 Insert the needle on line 1, level with the emerging thread on line 3. Bring the needle out on line 2 with the same stitch length as before. Pull the needle through.

4 Insert the needle on line 4, level with the emerging thread on line 2. Bring the needle out on line 3 with the same stitch length as before. Pull the needle through.

5 Insert the needle in line 5, level with the emerging thread on line 3. Bring the needle out on line 4 with the same stitch length as before. Pull the needle through.

6 Continue working back and forth across the lines to build up a line of stitches. Finish with a small stitch over the final feather stitch.

LONG-ARMED FEATHER STITCH
This stitch has a central ridge and is perfect for leaf veins.

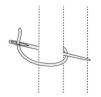 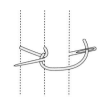 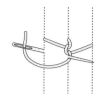

1 Use three guide lines. Bring the thread out on the middle line. Insert the needle on the left line, level with the emerging thread. Bring the needle out on the centre line, just below. Loop the thread under the needle point. Pull the needle through.

2 Insert the needle in the right line, level with the emerging thread. Bring the needle out just below on the centre line. Loop the thread under the needle point. Pull the needle through.

3 Insert the needle in the left line, level with the emerging thread. Bring the needle out just below, on the centre line. Loop the thread under the needle point. Pull the needle through.

4 Continue working stitches on alternate sides of the centre guide line, finishing with a small straight stitch over the final feather stitch.

DOUBLE LONG-ARMED FEATHER STITCH

BUTTONHOLED FEATHER STITCH
This stitch combination makes delicate fern fronds.

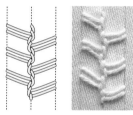 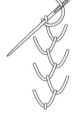   

To work double long-armed feather stitch, work as for regular long-armed feather stitch, but with two stitches on each alternating side.

1 Work a line of feather stitch. With a new thread, bring the thread just below the top of the centre arm of the uppermost feather stitch.

2 Without entering the fabric, work small buttonhole stitches down the feather arm towards its inner end.

3 Bring the thread out at the top of the next feather arm, and continue working buttonhole stitch along the subsequent feather arms.

SINGLE FEATHER STITCH
This stitch is also known as slanting buttonhole stitch.

1 Use two guide lines. Bring the thread out on the left line. Slightly lower, insert the needle diagonally in the right line, exiting on the left, and looping the thread under the needle point.

2 Pull the needle and thread through. Diagonally insert the needle in the right, and bring it out again on the left, with the needle point passing over the thread.

3 Repeat to build up a line of stitches. To finish, take a small stitch over the final feather stitch.

1 Use two guide lines. Bring the thread out on the right line. Insert the needle in the left line and bring it out a short distance below. Loop the thread under the needle point.

2 Pull the needle through. Insert it vertically in the right line, just below the previous stitch. Bring it out below, using the previous stitch length. Loop the thread under the needle point.

3 Pull the needle through. Insert it vertically in the left line, just below the previous stitch. Bring it out below, using the previous stitch length. Loop the thread under the needle point.

4 Repeat steps 2 and 3 to build up a line of stitching. Finish with a small straight stitch over the final closed feather stitch.

Upright feather stitch is also known as coral stitch. It is very similar to closed feather stitch.

1 Use two guide lines. Bring the thread out on the right line. Insert the needle in the left line level with the emerging thread. Bring the needle point out over the thread, a short way below.

2 Pull the needle through. Make a vertical stitch in the right line, starting level with the emerging thread and using the same stitch length as before. Loop the thread under the needle point.

3 Pull the needle through. Make a vertical stitch in the left line, using the same spacing and length as before. Loop the thread under the needle point.

4 Repeat steps 2 and 3 to build up a line of stitching. To finish, take a short stitch over the final stitch.

Fly stitch

1 Use three guides. Bring the thread out on the left line. Level with that, insert the needle in the right line. Bring it out a little way down on the centre line. Take the needle point over the thread.

2 Pull the needle through. A short distance below, insert the needle in the centre line. Using the same stitch length as before, bring it out on the left line.

3 Pull the needle through. Insert the needle in the right line and bring it out at the bottom of the previous fly stitch on the centre line. Take the needle point over the thread.

4 Continue to repeat steps 2 and 3 to build up a line of stitching. To finish, insert the needle in the centre line at the completion of a fly stitch.

❶ *By varying the width and length of the stitches, different effects are achieved.*

❶ *For a single fly stitch, work step 1, and finish with a small stitch at the bottom.*

French knot

Ideally you should use a straw (or milliner's) needle for french knots, as the eye of these needles is similar in width to the shaft. However, finding straw or milliner's needles with a large enough eye to fit Mountmellick thread can be very difficult. In these instances, the next best option is a large darner.

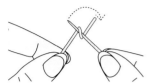  

enlarged

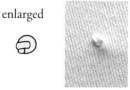

1 Bring the thread out of the fabric. Wind the thread around the needle once (or the number of times that are required). Take the needle point back over to where the thread emerges from the fabric.

2 Insert the needle point slightly to the right of the emerging thread (one or two fabric threads in between).

❶ *Do not take the needle all the way through the fabric.*

3 Holding the needle point below the fabric with your other hand, gently tighten the wrap(s) at the base of the needle shaft, so that they sit flush against the fabric.

❶ *This tightening will give a neat, compact knot.*

4 Gently pull the needle and thread through to the back of the fabric to complete the finished knot.

❶ *The more wraps a French knot has, the larger the knot will be. Top L–R: 1–4 wraps. Bottom L–R: 5–8 wraps.*

❶ *French knot blackberries (see page 73) have very large knots in their centres that look very untidy by themselves. As they are closely packed with other knots, this untidiness becomes insignificant.*

French knot clusters make great looking blackberries

Herringbone stitch

Herringbone stitch can be worked with large amounts of space between stitches (open), or with very little space between (closed), creating very different effects.

 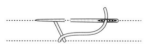 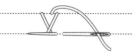 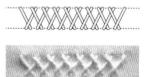

1 Use two guide lines. Bring the thread out on the top line. A little to the right, take a short stitch from right to left, on the bottom line. Pull the needle through.

2 Using the same spacing and stitch length as before, on the top line take a short stitch from right to left. Pull the needle through.

3 Using the same spacing and stitch length as before, take a short stitch in the bottom line, from right to left. Pull the needle through.

4 Repeat steps 2 and 3 to build up a line of stitching.

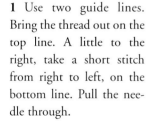

❶ *To work closed herringbone stitch, remove the spaces between the stitches.*

Indian filling

Indian filling is a self-couching stitch – the laid thread is also used for the couching.
The laid and couching stitches twist together to look like a single stitch.
Indian filling can be used more successfully than satin stitch for spanning long distances.

1 Use two guide lines.
❶ *Parallel sloped lines drawn within the stitching area can help to keep the stitching on the correct angle. Ensure the lines will be covered or can be washed out.*

2 Bring the thread out on the left line. Insert the needle on the right line and take a short stitch, angling the needle to emerge just above the thread. Pull the needle through.
❶ *Each stitch on the underside of the fabric is very short and the couching stitches on top of the fabric are relatively long.*

3 Insert the needle on the other side of the laid thread and bring the needle and thread out on the left line, just below the previous laid stitch. Once again keep the length of the stitch under the fabric very short.

4 Repeat steps 2 and 3, to build up an area of stitches.
❶ *Each couching stitch should start and finish in a different place to the previous one. This creates a random look.*

   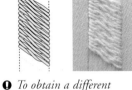 

❶ *Comparing the back and front of the stitching illustrates how little of the thread is on the back.*

❶ *The stitches should blend into each other and look as one stitch.*
❶ *Over longer distances and to curve the laid stitches, more than one couching stitch can be used.*

❶ *To obtain a different effect, bring the couching thread out below each laid thread. This will cause the threads to twist differently.*

Wild passionflower vines with tendrils are perfect for Mountmellick

Loop stitch

Loop stitch is a pretty stitch which makes a great leaf filling. It is worked from the bottom up.

 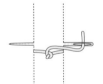 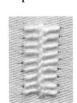

1 Use two guide lines. Bring the thread out centred between the two lines. A short distance up, insert the needle in the right line, and bring it out on the left line.

2 Pull the needle through. From the lower right, slide the needle under the first stitch, with the needle point going over the loop of thread. Pull the needle through.
❶ *Do not catch in any fabric.*

3 Using the same spacing as before, take a horizontal stitch from the right line to the left line.

4 Repeat steps 2 and 3 to build up a line of stitching. To finish, take a small stitch over the final loop section.

Mountmellick stitch

This stitch's origins are unknown as it is yet to be found on historical examples of Mountmellick embroidery.

1 Use two guide lines. Bring the thread out on the left line. A short way below, make a horizontal stitch from the right line to the left line. Pull the needle through.

2 From above right, insert the needle under the first stitch, without catching in any of the fabric, and pull the needle through.

3 Gently pull the thread downwards so that it fits snugly around the first stitch.

4 On the left line, take a stitch from the top of the first stitch down to the second stitch. Take the thread under the needle point. Pull the needle through.

❶ *This completes the first Mountmellick stitch.*

5 Using the same stitch length as before, horizontally insert the needle from the right line to the left line. Pull the needle through.

6 Repeat steps 2 and 3. Vertically insert the needle in the chain section above, emerging at the base of the stitching. Take the thread under the needle point.

7 Repeat steps 5 and 6 to build up a line of stitching. To finish, take a small stitch over the chain section.

❶ *Varying the width between the guide lines will alter the appearance of the stitching.*

ALTERNATING MOUNTMELLICK STITCH

 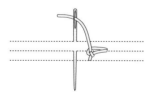 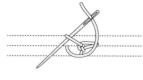 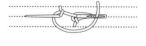

1 Use three guide lines. On the middle and right lines, work steps 1 to 4 as for Mountmellick stitch.

2 Turn the work 90 degrees clockwise. Using the same stitch length as before, insert the needle from the top line to the middle line.

❶ *The work is turned to aid comfortable needle insertion.*

3 From above, take the needle from right to left, under the diagonal stitch without catching in any of the fabric. Pull the needle through.

4 Insert the needle in the chain section of the previous Mountmellick stitch. Bring the needle out on the middle line at the far end of the stitch. Take the thread under the needle point.

5 Pull the needle through and gently tighten the stitch. Turn the work back to upright.

6 Continue working alternating stitches. Turn the work as needed.

Palestrina knot

This stitch is also known as double knot. It can be used for lines without 'arms' or as a filling with 'arms'.

1 Use one guide line. Bring the thread out on the line. A short way below, take a small stitch from right to left, from one side of the line to the other.

2 Slide the needle under the stitch from right to left.
❶ *Do not enter the fabric.*

3 Pull the thread through so that it fits snugly around the first stitch.

4 Insert the needle from the right, under the lower section of the first stitch. Take the needle over the thread. Pull the needle through.
❶ *Do not enter the fabric.*

5 Using the previous stitch length, take a short stitch from right to left, from one side of the line to the other.

6 Repeat steps 2 to 5 as needed. To finish, take a small stitch into the fabric at the end of step 4.

❶ *Altering the length of the vertical stitch taken in steps 1 and 5 (forming the 'arms') achieves different effects.*

Pomegranates are a favourite motif

Running stitch

Running stitch is used as a simple filling. The filling is usually worked first then outlined by a decorative stitch.

1 Bring the thread out on the line. Insert the needle point in and out several times on the line, entering or exiting a little further along the line each time.

2 Pull the needle and thread through so that the stitches lie flat against the fabric.
❶ *Do not pull too tightly or the fabric may pucker.*

3 Repeat as needed to fill the shape with lines of running stitch.

❶ *Stitches should be regular in length and evenly spaced. For a different effect, the stitches on top of the fabric can be consistently longer or shorter than those underneath.*

Satin stitch

When working satin stitch, the fabric should be held taut in a hoop or frame to avoid puckering.

1 Use two guides. Bring the thread out on the left line. Insert the needle level with this on the right line. Bring the needle out just below on the left line.

2 Pull the needle through. Work another stitch below the previous one.
❶ *Stitches are always made in the same direction. Do not work back and forth across the shape as the stitches will not sit properly.*

3 Continue working more stitches to fill the shape.

❶ *Pale or removable guide lines drawn within the stitching area can assist in keeping stitches parallel, or fanning to fit curves.*

Attractive tapered or rounded ends can be difficult to achieve. It is best to start in the centre and work outwards.

1 Begin at the centre and work towards one end.

2 At the end, taper the stitching to fit the shape.

3 Return to the centre and work out to the other end.

4 At the end, taper the stitching to fit the shape.

PADDED SATIN STITCH

Padded satin stitch uses layers of chain stitch for a firm, stable padding. Most satin stitch in Mountmellick work is padded. A hoop or frame must be used in order to minimise puckering. If you have trouble getting satin stitch to sit well, pad the satin stitch and it will make it much easier.

1 Outline the shape in chain stitch (see page 25) so that the outside edge of the chain stitch sits just inside the shape edge.

2 Fill the centre with additional rows of chain stitch.

❶ *Work additional layers of chain stitch over the first layer for extra height. Step them half a stitch width inwards so that each layer is slightly smaller than previous ones.*

3 Start working satin stitch at the centre, ready to work out to the sides. Bring the needle out at the edge of the shape, just under the edge of the chain stitching.

4 Insert the needle on the opposite side, just under the edge of the chain stitch.
❶ *This slightly conceals the stitch ends, smoothing the edge.*

5 Continue working satin stitch over the top of the chain stitch padding, out to one side.

6 Return to the centre and work out towards the other side.

7 Complete the satin stitching.

Spider web

Woven spider webs are infrequently used in Mountmellick embroidery.

1 Use an odd number of evenly spaced lines, radiating from a central point. Bring the thread out of the centre. Insert it into the end of a line, bringing it out at the centre again.
❶ *The length of the stitch determines the web's radius.*

2 Using the same stitch length, work around the circle to create the remainder of the foundation stitches.

3 Change to a tapestry needle. Bring the thread out close to the centre. Take the needle under one of the foundation stitches.
❶ *The needle should not be inserted into the fabric at any time during the weaving stage.*

4 Continue around the foundation stitches, weaving over and under, until the web is completely filled. To finish, take the needle through to the back.

Stem stitch

Closely related to outline stitch, the needle emerges above the line for stem stitch, and below for outline stitch.

1 Use one guide line. Bring the thread out on the line. Insert the needle a short distance to the right.

2 Pull the needle through. Leave the stitch sitting up. Bring the needle out on the line, above the stitch, and halfway along it.

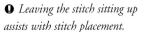

❶ *Leaving the stitch sitting up assists with stitch placement.*
❶ *Always bring the needle out on the same side of the stitching.*

3 Tighten so that the stitch sits flat. Make a new stitch the same length as before. Pull the needle through.

❶ *The stitches of the same length half overlap each other.*

4 Bring the needle out at the end of the first stitch. Pull the thread through to flatten the previous stitch.

5 Continue in the same way to build up a line of stitching.

OUTLINE STITCH

Work similarly to stem stitch, but bring the needle out below the stitch.

❶ *Outline stitch twists in the opposite direction to stem stitch.*

TURNING A SHARP CORNER

1 Work up to the corner and take the thread through to the back.

2 Bring the needle out at the far end of the next stitch, on the next side of the shape.

3 Insert the needle at the corner.

❶ *This backstitch fills the gap at the corner.*

4 Bring the needle out halfway along the stitch, and continue stitching forward as before.

PORTUGUESE STEM STITCH

1 Use one line. Bring the thread out on it. With the thread on the right, make a stitch. Bring the needle out halfway along the stitch.

2 Pull the needle through. With the thread at the top, slide the needle from right to left under the first stitch.

❶ *Do not catch in any fabric.*

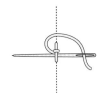

3 Take another stitch from right to left, below the previous one.

4 Using the same stitch length as before, insert the needle in the line. Bring it out at the first stitch's top. Pull the needle through.

5 Slide the needle under the top of the first stitch and under the current stitch.

❶ *Do not catch in any fabric.*

6 Take another stitch from right to left below the previous one.

7 Repeat steps 4 to 6 to continue stitching. To finish, take the thread to the back at the completion of step 6.

1 Bring the thread out above the last stem stitch, near the end. From below, slide the needle under the last two stitches.

❶ *Do not catch in any fabric.*

2 Continue whipping in the same way to build up a line of stitching. To finish, take the needle and thread through to the back next to the last stem stitch.

Morning glory is featured on the brush and comb bag on page 60.

Straight stitch

1 Bring the needle out and insert it at the end of the desired stitch length.

2 Pull the needle through so that the stitch sits flat on the fabric.

❶ *Stitches can be placed at any angle, and be of any length.*

Thorn stitch

Thorn stitch is unique to Mountmellick embroidery and is a feather stitch incorporating a french knot.

  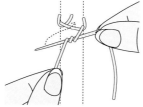 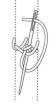

1 Use two guide lines. Bring the thread out between the lines. Vertically insert the needle into the left line, and bring it out a short way below. Take the thread under the needle point.

2 Pull the needle through. Using the same stitch length as previously, vertically insert the needle in the right line slightly lower than before. Take the thread under the needle point.

3 Pull the needle through. Wrap the thread around the needle three times. Take the needle point up and over the bottom of the previous stitch.

4 Insert the needle under the previous stitch, also taking in a tiny amount of the fabric beneath. Tighten the knot wraps around the needle. Take the thread under the needle point.

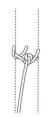   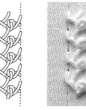

5 Pull the needle through to complete the french knot.

6 Insert the needle into the left line, bringing it out again a short distance below. Loop the thread under the needle point.

7 Continue to work steps 2 through 6, to build up a line of stitching. To finish, take a small stitch to end the french knot.

Trellis filling

Trellis stitch is created by laying threads and couching them with either half crosses or cross stitch.

1 Using even spacing, work parallel stitches back and forth across the shape.

2 Work stitches up and down to fill the shape, with the same spacing.

3 Over the intersections of the laid stitches, work a half cross.

❶ *All couching stitches lay in the same direction.*

4 When full crosses are required, work additional half crosses over the top of the first ones, in the opposite direction.

Vandyke stitch

1 Use four guide lines, numbered 1 to 4 from left to right. Bring the thread out on line 1. Slightly above, take a horizontal stitch from line 3 to line 2. Pull the needle through.

2 Insert the needle in line 4, level with the beginning of the first stitch. Bring the needle out on line 1, a little below the first stitch. Pull the needle through.

3 Slide the needle under the point where the two previous stitches cross over, and pull the needle through.

❶ *Do not enter the fabric.*

4 Insert the needle in line 4, level with where the thread emerges. Bring the needle out on line 1, using the same stitch length as before.

  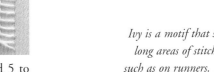

Ivy is a motif that suits long areas of stitching such as on runners.

5 Slide the needle under the lower parts of the previous stitch, and pull the needle through.

❶ *Do not enter the fabric.*

6 Repeat steps 4 and 5 to build up a line of stitching. To finish, take the needle to the back of the fabric at the completion of a stitch.

Waste knot

Use a waste knot to start a new thread when there is no stitching nearby. When there is stitching nearby, a new thread can be anchored in the back of that stitching.

1 Make a knot in the end of the thread.

2 From the front of the fabric, enter the needle about 8cm (3¹/₄in) away from the start of the stitching.

3 Begin stitching. When there is enough length to run a thread through the back, cut off the knot.

4 On the back of the fabric, run the thread under the back of the stitching. Trim any excess thread.

❶ *Finish all threads this way.*

Wheat ear stitch

  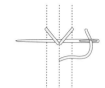

1 Use three guides. Bring the thread out on the left line. Insert the needle, lower, in the centre line. Bring the needle out on the right line, level with the first stitch's top. Pull the needle through.

2 Insert the needle into the centre line at the bottom of the first stitch. Bring the needle out again a short distance below. Pull the needle through.

3 Without entering the fabric, slide the needle under the previous two stitches, and pull it through.

4 Insert the needle where the thread emerged, and using the same stitch length as before, bring it out on the left line. Pull the needle through.

5 Insert the needle at the base of the previous stitch. Bring it out on the right line, level with the top of the previous stitch. Pull the needle through.

6 Repeating steps 2 to 5, build up a line of stitching. To finish, take the needle through to the back at the completion of step 3, finishing with a loop stitch.

❶ *Wheat ear stitches can also be used singly.*

....

Whipped cord button

This button is used to create blackberries and flower centres. It is firm and thick, and adds texture to the embroidery. The button is constructed separately and then attached to the fabric.

1 Take a doubled length of thread and twist it until it can be twisted no further. Fold the length in half, keeping the thread taut, and allow it to twist into a cord. Knot the loose ends together.

2 Thread a needle with a new thread, and tie a small, neat knot to anchor the beginning of the stitching.

3 Form a tight loop at the folded cord end. Take the needle through the doubled cord – not the centre. Pull the needle through.

4 Insert the needle up through the centre, with the thread passing around the doubled looped cord. Pull the needle through.

5 Wrap the cord beside the loop to begin the second circuit. Repeat the stitching, taking the needle up through the centre, and working around the loop.

6 Continue around the button, stitching through the outer two circuits of cord.

7 When the button reaches the desired size, take the remaining cord to the back and fasten it securely with a few back stitches. Trim any excess cord.

8 Attach the whipped cord button to the fabric by neatly whip stitching around the edge of the button, each time catching in some of the fabric. If the button pops up in the centre, take a small stitch through the centre to anchor it.

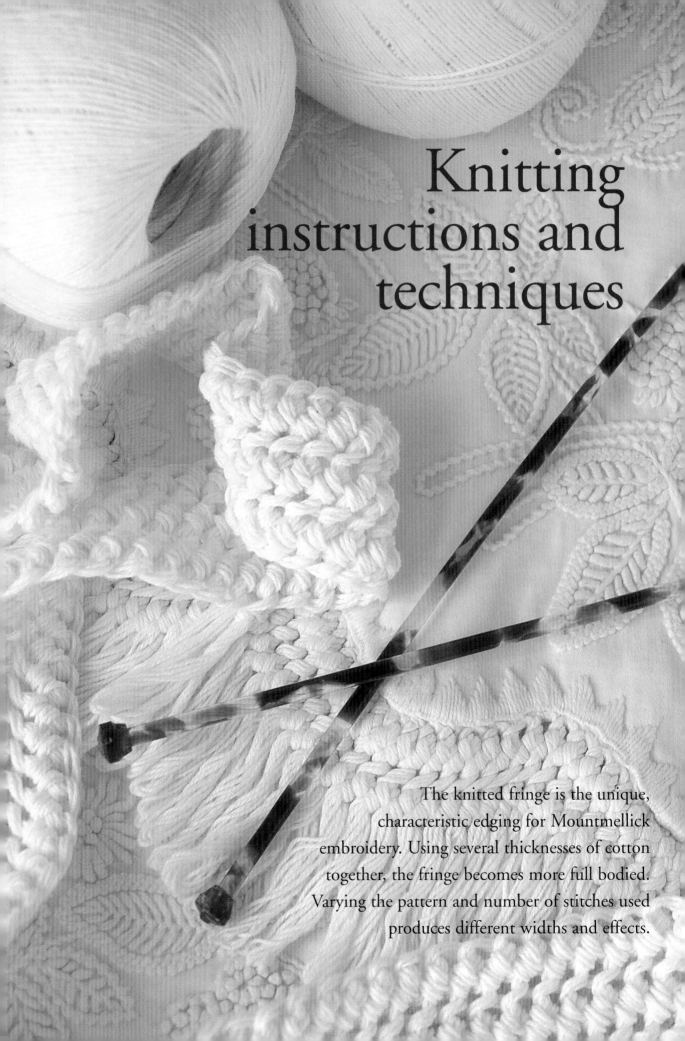

Knitting instructions and techniques

The knitted fringe is the unique, characteristic edging for Mountmellick embroidery. Using several thicknesses of cotton together, the fringe becomes more full bodied. Varying the pattern and number of stitches used produces different widths and effects.

Materials, equipment and preparation

To create the fringe, a strip is knitted to the length required and most of the stitches cast off. The remaining stitches are unravelled to create the fringe.

KNITTING NEEDLES

The knitting needles used for Mountmellick are 2.75, 3 and 3.25mm, equivalent to UK size 12, 11 and 10, and US size 2, 2-3 and 3. The thicker needles create a larger scale and more open lace and longer fringes. The thinner needles create smaller scale, less open lace, with shorter fringes.

It is advisable to use metal needles, as plastic, tortoiseshell or bamboo needles may break because of the bulk of the multiple threads. Because you are only knitting a narrow width, short needles (such as children's or double ended) are useful.

YARN

To create a full-bodied fringe, the knitting is done with multiple strands of yarn, for example, three, four or five strands. If possible, use the same thread as for the embroidery, as was traditionally done. If a number of different thicknesses of thread were used for the stitching, choose the one that was used most or the thickest one.

If you don't have access to large enough quantities of authentic Mountmellick thread, it may be preferable to use a non-shiny (non-mercerised) 4ply knitting cotton. Mercerised crochet cottons are not suitable as they are shiny. Try to choose something as similar as possible to the authentic threads: with a fine twist, that is not too furry, and with a dyelot that matches the embroidery as closely as possible.

This book's projects use 50gram balls of 4ply knitting cotton. This is specified so that anyone without access to the traditional supplies can still complete the projects.

Joining extra lengths of yarn

When joining new yarn, the join must be discreet (in case it is in the fringe) yet strong. Carefully and neatly tie a small, secure knot (of any type) to join the new yarn to the old one. With a hand on each side of the knot, gently pull to see if the knot holds firm or slips. If the knot slips, fasten it more securely. Trim the loose ends to neaten the join.

LEFT-HANDED KNITTING

The instructions provided are for right-handed knitters. Some left-handed people knit in the same manner as right-handed people. In this case you will not need to make any adaptations for being a left-hander. However, some left-handers reverse their knitting. If you knit left-handed, you will need to reverse the instructions by substituting 'left' for 'right' and vice versa, and reversing the diagrams. Some methods for this are described in the left-handed stitching notes on page 15.

KNITTED FRINGE METHODS

Because of all the variations possible (number of threads and stitches, size of needles, different patterns) it is wise to test the instructions before committing to any one method. Knit a short sample of 20 rows, cast off the stitches required and unravel the remaining stitches. This will help you to gauge whether the fringe length suits the size and scale of your piece. If you work up a number of these samples, make a note of the details, and keep them together for future reference.

In the project instructions, the number of rows required is not specified, as this will vary depending on one's knitting tension. Knit enough rows to fit around the entire embroidery, adding extra to ease into external corners.

Knitting techniques step-by-step

Making a slip knot

A slip knot is placed on the needle to begin knitting.

1 Make a large curve of yarn.

2 Make it into a loop by twisting the top of the curve down over the bottom part.

3 Twist the top of the loop down again.

4 Draw the long end of the yarn up and through the loop…

5 …thereby creating a loose slip knot.

6 Tighten the knot at the base of the slip knot.

Casting on

Use the cast on method described here as it produces a fringe loop of similar length to the other fringe loops. Other methods of casting on may produce fringe loops that are markedly different to the others.

1 Place the slip knot over the left needle.

2 Insert the right needle into the slip knot under the left needle.

3 Take the yarn around the right needle point from the back to the front.

4 Draw the right needle back within the stitches and bring it in front of the left needle.

5 Pull the right needle to the right to lengthen the loop that is around it.

6 Insert the left needle in the top of the new loop, with the left needle over the top of the right needle.

7 Slide the left needle further into the loop, and marginally tighten the loop around the needle.

8 Create additional stitches as needed, repeating from step 3.

Knitted fringe method 1

**This fringe has an inside edge with a narrow knitted ridge, then an open lacy area,
a wide ridge, an open area, another narrow ridge, then the fringe itself.
It requires a multiple of three stitches such as 9, 12, 15 etc.**

1 Cast on twelve stitches.
❶ *A single thread is shown here, but three or four strands of yarn together should be used when knitting a fringe.*

2 Insert the right needle in the front of the first stitch.

3 Take the thread around the right needle point from the back to the front.

4 Draw the right needle back and bring it in front of the left needle so that the new stitch is created.

5 Slide the left needle back so that the stitch comes off the needle.

6 Take the thread under the right needle from the back to the front.

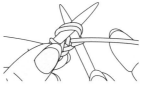

7 Insert the right needle in the front of the next two stitches on the left needle.

8 Take the thread around the right needle from the back to the front.

9 Draw the right needle back and bring it in front of the left needle so that the new stitch is created.

10 Slip the left needle out of the old stitches.
❶ *This completes the three stitch sequence.*

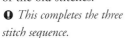

11 Repeat the sequence three times to complete the row.

12 Turn the work so that the right needle becomes the left needle, and repeat the pattern for each row.

13 Cast off 9 stitches. To create the fringe, unravel the remaining 3.

❶ *The unravelling process is akin to having a ladder or run in pantyhose. The unravelled stitches form the fringe.*

WRITTEN PATTERN – METHOD 1

Cast on 12 stitches (or multiple of 3) *(step 1)*.
Row 1: K1 *(steps 2–5)*, yfwd *(step 6)*, K2 tog *(steps 7–10)*. Repeat to end of row. (12 stitches.)
Row 2 and subsequent rows: Repeat first row.
Cast off 9 (the total number minus three) stitches.
Unravel the remaining 3.

Knitted fringe method 2

This fringe has an inside edge of an open lacy area, a ridge, an open area, another ridge, then the fringe itself. It requires a multiple of three stitches such as 9, 12, 15 etc.

1 Cast on nine stitches.
❶ *A single thread is shown here, but three or four strands of yarn together should be used when knitting a fringe.*

2 Take the thread across the front of the right needle.

3 Insert the right needle in the front of the first two stitches.

4 Wind the thread around the right needle from the back to the front.

5 Slide the right needle back and then in front of the left needle to bring the new stitch through.

6 Slide the right needle further into the stitch, and the left needle out of the old stitches.

7 Insert the right needle in the front of the next stitch on the left needle.

8 Take the thread around the right needle from the back to the front.

9 Draw the right needle back and bring it in front of the left needle so that the new stitch is created.

10 Slip the left needle out of the old stitch.
❶ *This completes the three stitch sequence.*

11 Bring the yarn forward in front of the right needle.

12 Insert the needle in the front of the next two stitches.

13 Starting from Step 4, repeat the steps as needed to the end of the row, finishing with Step 10.

14 Turn the work so that the right needle becomes the left needle, and repeat the pattern for each row.

15 Cast off 6 stitches. To create the fringe, unravel the remaining 3.
❶ *The unravelling process is akin to having a ladder or run in pantyhose. The unravelled stitches form the fringe.*

WRITTEN PATTERN – METHOD 2

Cast on 9 stitches (or multiple of 3) *(step 1)*.
Row 1: yfwd *(step 2)*, K2 tog *(steps 3–6)*, K1 *(steps 7–10)*.
Repeat to end of row. (9 stitches.)
Row 2 and subsequent rows: Repeat first row.
Cast off 6 (the total number minus three) stitches.
Unravel the remaining 3.

Knitted fringe method 3

This knitted fringe is the one that is featured on most historic examples of Mountmellick embroidery, and is therefore probably the most authentic. It is created with six stitches and is always purled rather than knitted. It creates a neat, compact fringe which curves well around corners.

1 Cast on six stitches.
❶ *A single thread is shown here, but three or four strands of yarn together should be used when knitting a fringe.*

2 Take the thread across the front of the right needle.

3 Wind the thread around the needle once.

4 Slip the first stitch purlwise, from the left needle to the right, and off the left.

5 Insert the right needle from the right (purlwise), into the front of the next stitch.

6 Take the thread around the back of the right needle from the right to the left.

7 Draw back the right needle and take it under the part of the stitch still on the left needle.

8 Take the right needle through to behind the left needle.

9 Allow the stitch to come off the left needle.

10 Lift the slipped stitch on the right needle up with the left needle.

11 Take it over the purled stitch, and off the right needle.

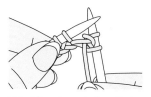

12 Slip the stitch off the left needle.
❶ *This completes the two stitch sequence.*

13 From the front, wind the thread around the needle so that the thread comes to the front again.

14 Cycle through the remaining steps from step 4 onwards, repeating twice to complete the row.

15 Turn the work so that the right needle becomes the left needle, and repeat the pattern for each row.

16 Cast off 4 stitches, purlwise. To create the fringe, unravel the remaining 2.
❶ *The unravelling process is akin to having a ladder or run in pantyhose. The unravelled stitches form the fringe.*

WRITTEN PATTERN – METHOD 3

❶ *This fringe is always purled.*
Cast on 6 stitches *(step 1)*.
Row 1: yrn *(steps 2–3)*, sl 1 P-wise *(step 4)*, P1 *(steps 5–9)*, psso *(steps 10–12)*. Repeat to end of row. (6 stitches.)
Row 2 and subsequent rows: Repeat first row.
Cast off 4 stitches. Unravel the remaining 2.

Casting off

Knit cast off is shown. To cast off purlwise, purl each stitch instead of knitting them.

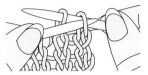

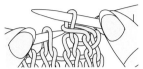

3 Knit the next stitch and lift the previous one over the top of it and off the needle. Repeat for subsequent stitches until only one remains on the needle.

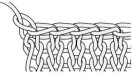

1 Knit the first two stitches of the row. Slip the point of the left needle into the first stitch of the row.

2 Using the left needle, lift the first stitch over the second stitch, and off the end of the right needle.

4 Cut the yarn and slip the end through the last stitch. Tighten. Neatly sew the end into the knitted fabric.

Attaching the fringe

When the fringe has been completed it can be sewn to the edge of the embroidery piece. The knitted fringe is sewn only to the buttonhole edging, not to the fabric itself.

1 Neatly stitch the ends of the fringe together with the same yarn as was used for the knitting.

2 Spread the knitting evenly around the edge of the embroidered piece, with the fringe on the outer edge.
❶ *Where possible, position the join in the fringe where it is most insignificant.*

3 Use pins or safety pins to temporarily attach the knitting to the fabric surrounding the embroidery.
❶ *Ensure there is extra to be eased into curves and corners.*

4 Fasten the thread in the back of the buttonhole stitch. Bring the needle out through the rolled edge of the buttonhole.

5 Bring the needle up through a loop at the edge of the knitted fringe.

6 Enter the needle into the edge of the buttonhole a little way along. Bring the needle out in the next loop on the edge of the knitted fringe.

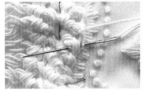

7 Continue around the edge, using a neat whip stitch to attach the fringe.
❶ *Ease extra fullness into the corners and around curves so that the knitting will sit flat.*

8 When the fringe is attached, remove the pins.

CUTTING OUT THE WORK

❶ *Take great care not to catch the scissors in the stitching or the fringe.*

1 Working from the back, carefully and slowly cut as close as possible to the edge of the buttonhole stitching without damaging it.

2 Continue around until all the fabric has been cut away. Remove the trimmed fabric.

Projects
with traditional
applications

Mountmellick embroidery is very sturdy because of the use of heavy fabric and bold stitching. This sturdiness means that it is entirely suitable for use on everyday household items; it is not just an embroidery style for special occasions. After use it can be boiled clean to restore it to pristine condition.

The articles to which Mountmellick embroidery was traditionally applied include nightdress cases, brush and comb bags, bedspreads, pillow shams, table centres and toilet mats (doilies).

Leaf sampler

This sampler is an ideal starter project as it shows how to use and combine many of the Mountmellick stitches. Three thicknesses of thread familiarise stitchers with how thread weight affects scale. These leaves can be used as they appear here, or can be adapted to other shapes, and the stitches mixed and matched for other projects. Many of these combinations are taken from historic Mountmellick embroidery pieces.

RATING
Beginner

SIZE
13 x 23cm (5 x 9¹/₁in)

MATERIALS
- *30 x 40cm (12 x 16in) cotton satin jean*
- *No.2 Mountmellick thread*
- *No.3 Mountmellick thread*
- *No.4 Mountmellick thread*
- *No.22 chenille needle*
- *No.3 darner needle*

STITCHES USED
Bokhara couching, bullion, buttonhole, cable chain, cable plait, coral knot, cretan, detached buttonhole filling, detached chain, double feather, feather, french knot, indian filling, long-armed feather, overcast cable plait, padded satin, palestrina knot, satin, stem, straight, thorn, trellis, whipped buttonhole.

EMBROIDERY

❶ *Trace the pattern (p50) onto the fabric. The leaves are numbered 1 to 21. Use the chenille needle except where otherwise specified. Mount the fabric in a hoop so that it is drum tight.*

Leaf 1 Using No.4 thread, work the centre in cretan stitch. Stitch the border in two separate lines of cable plait stitch, with one butting the other at the leaf points.

Leaf 2 Use No.3 thread. From the leaf tip work double feather stitch down the centre. Create a line of french knots (three wraps, darner needle) for the outline.

Leaf 3 With No.3 thread, work satin stitch for each leaf side coming to a point at the top of the leaf. Over the top, work evenly spaced bullions with No.4 thread and the darner needle.

Leaf 4 Starting at the leaf tip using No.2 thread, work the centre vein in feather stitch, with veins branching off to the side where the leaf widens. Stitch the border in cable plait stitch, with the ends butting at the ends of the leaf.

Leaf 5 In No.3 thread, work the centre of the leaf as a couched trellis, and the border as cable chain stitch.

Leaf 6 Use No.3 thread and the darner needle to work the veins as evenly spaced bullions coming to a point at

Leaf 1   *Leaf 2*

Leaf 3   *Leaf 4*

Leaf 5   *Leaf 6*

the top of the leaf. Work the inner border in tightly packed coral knot stitch and then an outer border of short straight stitches radiating from the coral knot stitch.

Leaf 7 Work each side of the leaf using No. 3 thread and indian filling.

Leaf 8 Using No. 3 thread, from the tip, work feather stitch in the centre. Work an inner border of palestrina knot stitch. Stitch an outer border of buttonhole, with the rolled edge towards the inside of the leaf. Taper the buttonhole at the leaf tip, and curve it around at the base.

Leaf 9 With No. 4 thread, fill each half of the leaf with two layers of chain stitch padding. Over the top of the padding, use No. 2 thread to work satin stitch down each side of the leaf.

Leaf 10 Using No. 4 thread, work coral knot stitch for the outline and centre vein. Scatter french knots (three wraps, darner needle) to fill each side of the leaf.

Leaf 11 With No. 4 thread, stitch the centre using palestrina knot with long arms. Make a border of whipped buttonhole stitch, with the rolled section at the edge of the leaf. Curve the buttonhole at the top and bottom of the leaf, rather than tapering it to the points.

Leaf 12 Use No. 3 thread. From the tip, work the centre vein in long-armed feather stitch. Work the outline in tightly packed coral knot stitch.

Leaf 13 Starting at the leaf tip each time, and using No. 2 thread, buttonhole stitch down each side of the leaf, with the rolled edges at the centre vein.

Leaf 14 Starting at the tip, work the leaf in open cretan stitch, using No. 4 thread.

Leaf 15 Using No. 3 thread, work stem stitch outlines, and scattered french knots (three wraps, darner needle) to fill the leaf.

Leaf 16 Work bokhara couching with No. 4 thread, lining up the couching stitches down the centre vein.

Leaf 17 Using No. 2 thread, work detached buttonhole filling in the centre of the leaf, taking care to keep tension even throughout. With No. 4 thread, work the outline in overcast cable plait, with the overcasting outermost.

Leaf 18 Using No. 3 thread, work satin stitch to fill each side of the leaf, with alternate stitches stepped in and out.

Leaf 19 With No. 3 thread, from the tip, fill the centre with long-armed feather stitch. Work an inner border of coral knot stitch. Using the darner needle, stitch the outer border in alternating bullions and straight stitch.

Leaf 20 Using No. 3 thread and starting at the leaf tip, work the centre vein in thorn stitch. Stitch an outline of palestrina knot stitch.

Leaf 21 With No. 4 thread, work a layer of chain stitch padding in the inner part of each side of the leaf (see diagram). Use the No. 3 thread to work detached chain stitch, with the chain section of each stitch stretching over padding, and the anchoring section of the stitch only in the outer edge area.

FINISHING

When all the embroidered leaves are complete, soak to remove the guide lines and wash it to whiten. Press. Frame the embroidery if desired, or use as a reference for future Mountmellick stitching. ❦

Leaf 7   *Leaf 8*

Leaf 9   *Leaf 10*

Leaf 11   *Leaf 12*

Leaf 13   *Leaf 14*

Leaf 15   *Leaf 16*

Leaf 17   *Leaf 18*

Leaf 19   *Leaf 20*

Leaf 21

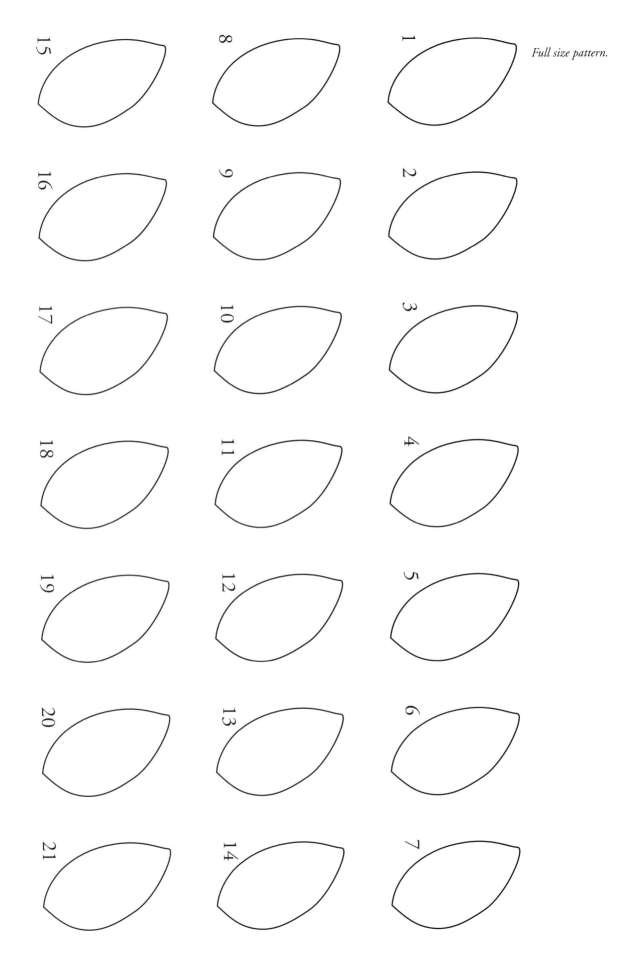

Full size pattern.

15   8   1

16   9   2

17   10   3

18   11   4

19   12   5

20   13   6

21   14   7

Blackberry doily

The scalloped edge on this doily features the fringe most often used on antique Mountmellick embroidery.

EMBROIDERY

❶ *Trace the pattern (p52) onto the fabric. The motifs are numbered 1 to 8. Use the chenille needle except where otherwise specified. Mount the fabric in a hoop so that it is drum tight.*

Shorter stem Work the stem in coral knot stitch.

Flowers 1 For the petals, work satin stitch over a layer of chain stitch padding. Work a single french knot (three wraps, darner needle) in the flower centre.

Leaves 2 Outline the leaves in cable plait stitch, starting at the tip, and curving around at the bottom. From the tip, work feather stitch down the leaf vein.

Leaves 3 Work detached chain stitch up the leaf sides. Angle them so that the stitch at the tip lies along the centre vein.

Longer stem Work stem stitch.

Leaves 4 Outline in palestrina knot stitch. From the leaf tips, fill the leaves with long-armed feather stitch.

Leaves 5 Divide the leaves into sections. Start each section at the leaf edge and work buttonhole towards the centre. Work whipped stem stitch for the centre vein.

Flowers 6 Use the darner. Work radiating bullions for the petals, with three french knots (three wraps) in the centre.

Leaves 7 Outline the leaves in coral knot stitch. From the tip, work Mountmellick stitch down the centre vein.

Fruit 8 Work as for small blackberries (page 73) using the darner needle.

Edging Work buttonhole stitch angled to fit the scallops.

FINISHING
When all embroidery is complete, soak to remove guide lines and wash to whiten. Press.

KNITTED FRINGE
Use four strands of knitting cotton together. Cast on 6 stitches. With Method 3 (page 45), knit a length to go around the doily. Cast off 4 stitches. Unravel the remaining 2.

Using a neat whip stitch, stitch the ends of the knitting together. Attach the fringe to the buttonhole edging of the doily, easing extra into the curves. Carefully cut the embroidery from the surrounding fabric. ❧

RATING
Beginner
SIZE
17 x 24cm (6¾ x 9½in) excluding fringe
MATERIALS
- *30 x 40cm (12 x 16in) cotton satin jean*
- *No.3 Mountmellick thread*
- *No.22 chenille needle*
- *No.3 darner needle*
- *4 x 50 gram balls 4ply knitting cotton, white*
- *2.75mm (UK 12, US 2) metal knitting needles*
STITCHES USED
Bullion, buttonhole, cable plait, coral knot, detached chain, feather, french knot, long-armed feather, mountmellick, padded satin, palestrina knot, stem, whipped stem.

Flowers 1   *Leaves 2*

Leaves 3   *Leaves 4*

Leaves 5   *Flowers 6*

Leaves 7   *Fruit 8*

Full size pattern.

Honeysuckle doily

This small doily is an ideal beginner's project, using only a few easily mastered stitches.

RATING
Beginner

SIZE
16cm (6¼in) diameter,
excluding fringe

MATERIALS
- *22 x 22cm (8½ x 8½in)*
  cotton satin jean
- *No.3 Mountmellick thread*
- *No.22 chenille needle*
- *No.3 darner needle*
- *3 x 50 gram balls 4 ply*
  knitting cotton, white
- *3.25mm (UK 10, US 3)*
  metal knitting needles

STITCHES USED
Bullion, buttonhole, cording,
long-armed feather, padded
satin, stem.

EMBROIDERY

❶ *Trace the entire pattern (p54) onto the fabric. All embroidery is worked with the chenille needle unless otherwise indicated. Mount the fabric in a hoop so that it is drum tight.*

Flowers Work the flowers in buttonhole stitch. Stitch the stamens in stem stitch, with a second row near the top for the thickening of the stamens.

Buds Stitch the buds in padded satin stitch, with two layers of chain stitch padding.

Stem Work the stem in cording stitch.

Right leaf Work the leaf in long-armed feather stitch, starting at the tip.

Left leaf Stitch the leaf in bullion stitch using the darner needle, angling the bullions so that the one at the leaf tip lies along the centre vein.

Border Stitch the border in cording stitch.

Edging Work the edging in buttonhole stitch.

Flowers and buds

Right leaf

53

Full size pattern.

Left leaf

Edging and border

FINISHING

When all embroidery is complete, soak to remove guide lines and wash to whiten. Press.

KNITTED FRINGE

Using three strands of knitting cotton together, cast on 6 stitches. Using Method 2 on page 44, knit a length that measures the same as the buttonhole edging of the doily. Cast off 3 stitches and unravel the remaining 3.

Using a neat whip stitch, stitch the ends of the knitting together. Attach the fringe to the buttonhole edging of the doily, easing extra into the corners. Carefully cut the embroidery from the surrounding fabric. ❦

Shamrock and lily doily

This square scalloped doily features a stem of lilies surrounded by scattered shamrocks.

RATING
Beginner

SIZE
28 x 28cm (11 x 11in), excluding fringe

MATERIALS
- *38 x 38cm (15 x 15in) cotton satin jean*
- *No.3 Mountmellick thread*
- *No.22 chenille needle*
- *No.3 darner needle*
- *3 x 50 gram balls 4ply knitting cotton, white*
- *3.25mm (UK 10, US 3) metal knitting needles*

STITCHES USED
Bullion, buttonhole, cable chain, coral knot, cording, double bullion, double feather, feather, french knot, long armed feather, padded buttonhole, padded satin, satin, single feather, stem, thorn.

EMBROIDERY

❶ *Trace the pattern (p57) onto the fabric. The motifs are numbered. All embroidery is worked with the chenille needle unless otherwise specified. Mount the fabric in a hoop so that it is drum tight.*

Edging Work a line of chain stitch centred between the two lines of the edging. Work buttonhole stitch over the top of the chain stitch padding, fanning the buttonhole stitches to fit the curves and points. The buttonhole rolled edge forms the edge of the doily.

Leaf 1 Work an outline of padded satin stitch (one layer of chain stitch padding), shaping it as shown in the photo, below. There is no stitching down the centre vein.

Leaf 2 Work the outline in coral knot stitch. Stitch an inner border in stem stitch. From the leaf tip, work the centre vein in double feather stitch.

Leaf 3 Stitch the border in single feather stitch with the rolled section at the edge of the leaf. From the leaf tip, work the centre vein in feather stitch.

Leaf 4 Outline the leaf with closely spaced french knots (three wraps, using darner needle). Work the centre vein in cable chain stitch. Work slanting bullions down each side of the centre vein using the darner needle.

Leaf 5 Stitch the outline in cable chain. From the leaf tip, work the centre vein in thorn stitch.

Leaf 6 Work the border in satin stitch, with every second stitch indented from the edge. Work the centre vein as a line of french knots (three wraps, darner needle).

Leaf 7 Outline the leaf in closely spaced coral knot stitch. Work the vein from the tip, in long-armed feather stitch.

Leaf 8 Using the darner needle, work bullions on each side of the leaf, coming to a point at the leaf tip.

Lily 1 Work the stamens and style in stem stitch. Using the darner needle, work double bullions for each of the six anthers, and five bullions for the stigma as shown. Outline the petals using padded buttonhole with one layer of padding and positioning the rolled edge as shown in the photo. Scatter french knots (three wraps, darner needle) within the petals.

Edging

Leaves 1 to 4

Leaves 5 to 8

Lily 1

Lily 2 Work the stamens and style in stem stitch. Stitch the anthers and stigma with padded satin (one layer of padding). Outline the petals in a wavy buttonhole stitch, with the waves innermost on the petals. Scattered the petals with detached chain stitches.

Stems Use cording stitch to work the stems.

Shamrocks Use bullion stitch for the shamrock stalks (darner needle). The leaves are worked in padded satin stitch, using the method as follows: work a line of chain stitch around the edge of the leaves. Using a slanting satin stitch, work up one side of the leaf to the

Lily 2

Stems

Shamrocks

rounded end, fanning the satin stitch around. Work down the other side in a slanting satin stitch to mirror the opposite half.

Pattern shown at 50% of full size. Photocopy onto A3 paper at 200% to obtain the full size pattern.

FINISHING
When all embroidery is complete, soak to remove guide lines and wash to whiten. Press.

KNITTED FRINGE
With three strands of the knitting cotton together, cast on 9 stitches. Using Method 1 on page 43, knit a length long enough to go around the mat. Cast off 6 stitches and unravel the remaining 3.

Neatly stitch the ends of the knitting together. Sew the fringe to the edge of the doily, taking small whip stitches through the rolled buttonhole edge and easing extra fullness into the corners and curves. Carefully cut the embroidery from the surrounding fabric.

Wheat mat

This mat features favourite Mountmellick stitches, such as bullion, padded satin, cable plait and cable chain stitches. The outer edge has a wide knitted fringe.

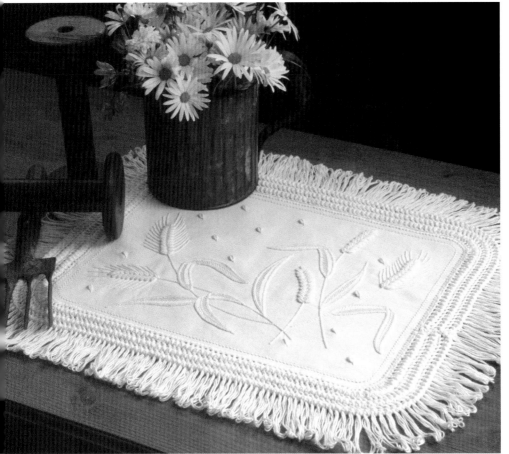

Leaves, stems and powdering

Wheat

Wheat (without spikes)

Border and edging

RATING
Intermediate

SIZE
32 x 41cm (12½ x 16¼ in), excluding fringe

MATERIALS
- *40 x 50cm (15¾ x 19¾ in) cotton satin jean*
- *No.2 Mountmellick thread*
- *No.22 chenille needle*
- *No.14 darner needle*
- *3 x 50 gram balls 4ply knitting cotton, white*
- *3.25mm (UK 10, US 3) metal knitting needles*

STITCHES USED
Bullion, cable chain, cable plait, herringbone, long-armed feather, stem, stepped buttonhole, straight.

EMBROIDERY
❶ *Trace the pattern (p59) onto the fabric. All embroidery is worked with the chenille needle except where specified. Mount the fabric in a hoop so that it is drum tight.*

Leaves Work the outlines in cable plait stitch. Where the leaves fold, work stem stitch along the folded edge. Fill each leaf with long-armed feather stitch, starting at the tips.

Stems Stitch the stems using cable chain stitch.

Wheat Using the darner needle, work the wheat grains as double bullions – two bullions worked side by side, with ends meeting. Work the spikes in stem stitch.

Powdering Work double bullions with a short tail of straight stitch.

Border Between the inner two lines around the pattern edge, work open herringbone.

Edging Between the outermost two lines on the pattern, work stepped buttonhole.

FINISHING
When all embroidery is complete, soak to remove guide lines and wash to whiten. Press.

KNITTED FRINGE

With three strands of knitting cotton together, cast on 12 stitches. Using Method 2 on page 44, knit a length long enough to go around the mat. Cast off 9 stitches and unravel the remaining 3.

Neatly stitch the knitting ends together. Sew the fringe to the mat's edge, taking small whip stitches through the buttonhole edge and easing extra fullness into the corners. Carefully cut the embroidery from the surrounding fabric. ❦

Pattern shown at 50% of full size. Photocopy the top half and the bottom half onto A3 pages at 200%. Match the dotted lines and tape them together to obtain the full size pattern.

Morning glory brush and comb bag

Brush and comb bags and larger, more rectangular bags used as nightdress cases
were popular traditional Mountmellick embroidery projects.

RATING
Intermediate

SIZE
*19 x 27 cm (7½ x 10½ in),
excluding fringe*

MATERIALS
- *Piece A: 30 x 42 cm (12 x 17 in) cotton satin jean*
- *Piece B: 30 x 50 cm (12 x 20 in) cotton satin jean*
- *No. 3 Mountmellick thread*
- *No. 4 Mountmellick thread*
- *No. 22 chenille needle*
- *No. 3 darner needle*
- *3 x 50 gram balls 4 ply knitting cotton, white*
- *3.25 mm (UK 10, US 3) metal knitting needles*

STITCHES USED
Bullion, buttonhole, cable chain, cable plait, chain, coral knot, detached buttonhole filling, detached chain, french knot, padded satin, palestrina knot, stem.

EMBROIDERY

❶ *Trace both patterns (p62) for the bag, including the edges, onto the fabric. Work all stitching with the chenille needle and No. 3 thread unless otherwise indicated. Mount the fabric in a hoop so that it is drum tight.*

Piece A

Leaf 1 The outline is stitched in cable plait stitch. Work the veins in bullion stitch with the darner needle.

Leaf 2 Using No. 4 thread, work detached chain stitch down each side of the leaf. The arms of the chain stitches point towards the edge of the leaf, with one arm shorter than the other, as shown above. Fan the arms out towards the tip to create the leaf point.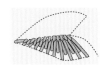

Leaf 3 Work the outline in coral knot stitch. Using No. 4 thread, stitch the veins in cable chain stitch.

Leaf 4 Work the entire leaf in buttonhole stitch with the rolled edge outermost, leaving gaps for the veins.

Flower Fill the petals in detached buttonhole filling, and outline with stem stitch. With the darner needle, work a short bullion as the flower centre. Work the flower base in padded satin stitch (two layers of chain stitch padding). Outline the sepals in stem stitch.

Stems Work each stem in palestrina knot stitch.

Piece B

Leaf on bag flap Stitch the outline with two rows of tightly packed french knots (three wraps, darner needle), and the veins in chain stitch.

KNITTED FRINGE

Using three strands of knitting cotton together, cast on 6 stitches. Using Method 2 on page 44, knit two lengths: one for the sides and bottom of the bag, and a second one to edge the entire flap section. For both, cast off 3 stitches and unravel the remaining 3.

CONSTRUCTION

❶ *Make sure that all the embroidery is on the front when the bag is constructed.*

Buttonhole stitch around the edge of the flap on piece B. Fold down the flap along the fold line as marked on the pattern. Work buttonhole stitch along the fold.

Piece A leaf 1 and stem

Piece A leaf 2

Piece A leaf 3

Piece A leaf 4

Work buttonhole stitch across the top of piece A.

Match the dots on pieces A and B. From the front, buttonhole the two layers of fabric together. Begin at one dot and work around the outer edge of the bag to the other dot.

When all embroidery is complete, soak to remove guide lines and wash to whiten. Press.

Using a neat whip stitch, attach the shorter length of fringe to the top and sides of the flap. Attach the longer fringe to the outer edge of the bag, starting and finishing at the dots on each side. Carefully cut the embroidery from the surrounding fabric. ❦

Flower and stems

Piece B leaf

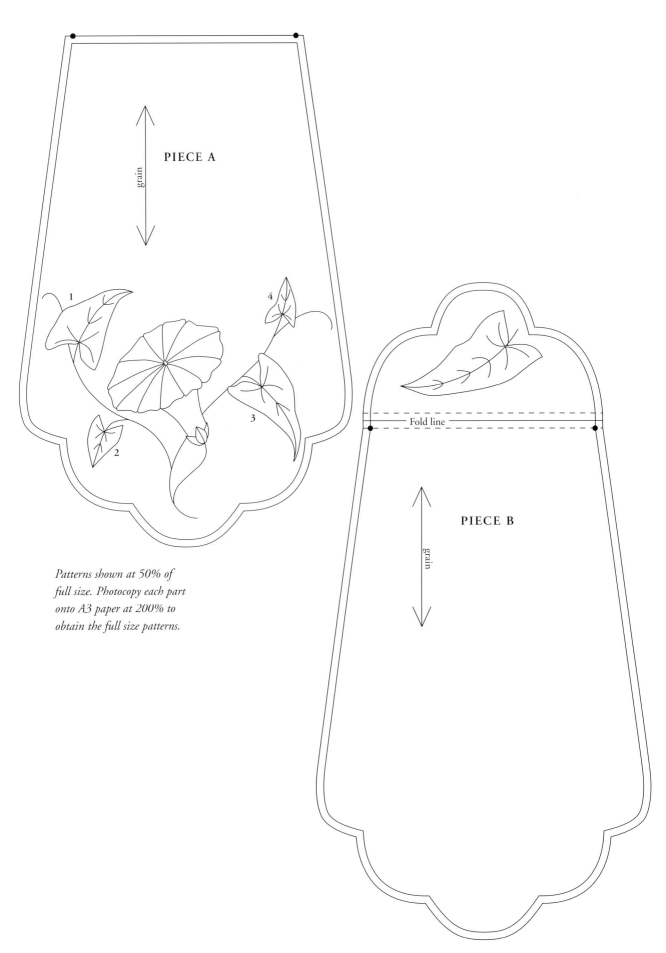

PIECE A

grain

PIECE B

grain

Fold line

Patterns shown at 50% of full size. Photocopy each part onto A3 paper at 200% to obtain the full size patterns.

Oval dogrose doily

Featuring a buttonhole fringe instead of the regular knitted fringe, this scalloped oval doily uses a wide variety of stitches.

RATING

Intermediate

SIZE

29 x 41 cm (11½ x 16¼ in), excluding fringe

MATERIALS

- *35 x 45cm (14 x 18in) cotton satin jean*
- *No. 2 Mountmellick thread*
- *No. 3 Mountmellick thread*
- *No. 4 Mountmellick thread*
- *No. 22 chenille needle*
- *No. 3 darner needle*

STITCHES USED

Bullion, buttonhole, cable chain, cable plait, chain, coral knot, cording, cretan, detached buttonhole filling, detached chain, feather, locked buttonhole fringe, long-armed feather, mount-mellick, overcast cable plait, padded buttonhole, padded satin, palestrina knot, por-tuguese stem, seeding, stem, vandyke, wheat ear.

EMBROIDERY

❶ *Trace the pattern (p65) onto the fabric. Use the chenille needle and No. 3 thread for all embroidery, except where otherwise indicated. Mount the fabric in a hoop so that it is drum tight.*

Dogrose 1 Using No. 4 thread, outline the petals in cable chain stitch. Using No. 3 thread, stitch the flower centre in detached chain stitch, with one arm of each chain stitch twice as long as the other. Using the darner needle, stitch the stamens in bullions.

Dogrose 2 Stitch the outline of the petals using padded satin stitch (one layer of chain stitch padding). Fill the middle of the flower with seeding. Using the darner needle, stitch a circular overwrapped bullion in the centre, as shown right.

Dogrose 3 Stitch the petals in padded buttonhole stitch (one layer of chain stitch padding). Change to No. 2 thread. Inside the petals, stitch a circle of palestrina knot stitch. In the centre of the flower, stitch a small circle of chain stitch.

Opening flower Fill the petals with detached buttonhole filling, and outline them in stem stitch. Using the darner needle, stitch the sepals in bullion stitch. Work the flower stem in palestrina knot stitch.

Flower buds Stitch the buds in padded satin stitch (one layer of chain stitch padding). Using the darner needle, work the spikes on the buds as bullions.

Leaves 4 Work the stem in cording stitch. Using No. 4 thread, stitch the leaves in cre-tan stitch.

Leaf 5 Outline the leaf in portuguese stem stitch. Stitch two lines of mountmellick stitch, facing away from each other, about 2mm (¹/₁₂in) apart.

Dogrose 1

Dogrose 2

Dogrose 3

Leaves 6 Outline the leaves in chain stitch. Stitch the veins in wheat ear stitch. Work the stems in cording stitch.

Leaves 7 Stitch the leaves in long-armed feather stitch and the stems in cording stitch.

Leaves 8 Using No. 4 thread, stitch the leaves in vandyke stitch. Outline the leaves in stem stitch using No. 2 thread. Work the stems in palestrina knot stitch using No. 3 thread.

Leaves 9 Using No. 2 thread, outline the leaves in cable plait stitch, with overcasting on the outside. Using No. 4 thread, stitch the stems and leaf veins using palestrina knot stitch, using long arms to fill the leaves.

Leaves 10 Outline the leaves in tightly spaced coral knot stitch. Using the darner needle, fill the leaves with bullions along either side of the vein. Stitch the stems in palestrina knot stitch. Work a single chain stitch at the base of the leaf stem for the small leaf.

Stem 11 Work the main stem in feather stitch. Work the secondary stems in cording stitch.

Stem 12 Work the main stem in cable plait stitch. Use No. 4 thread at the base of the stem below Dogrose 3 and above the flower use No. 3 thread. Work the secondary stems in palestrina knot stitch using No. 3 thread.

Edging Stitch around the edge of the doily in locked buttonhole fringe.

FINISHING

When all embroidery is complete, soak to remove guide lines and wash to whiten. Press. Cut the embroidery from the surrounding fabric, taking extra care not to cut through any of the buttonhole fringe. ❦

Opening flower

Flower buds

Leaves 4

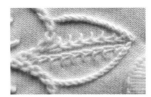

Leaf 5

Leaves 6

Leaves 7

Leaves 8

Leaves 9

Leaves 10

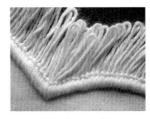

Buttonhole fringe edging

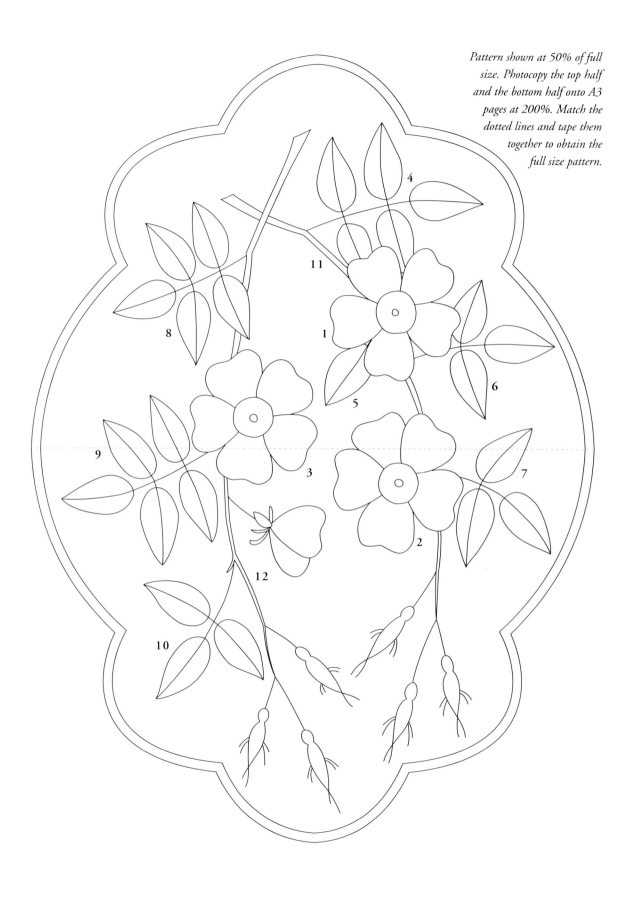

Pattern shown at 50% of full size. Photocopy the top half and the bottom half onto A3 pages at 200%. Match the dotted lines and tape them together to obtain the full size pattern.

Lily and forget-me-not nightdress case

Keep your pyjamas or nightdress fresh in this pretty case each day.

RATING
Intermediate

SIZE
30 x 40cm (12 x 16in), excluding fringe

MATERIALS
- *Piece A: 30 x 50cm (12 x 20in) cotton satin jean*
- *Pieces B and C: 40 x 50cm (16 x 20in) cotton satin jean (2 pieces)*
- *No.3 Mountmellick thread*
- *No.22 chenille needle*
- *No.3 darner needle*
- *4 x 50 gram balls 4ply knitting cotton, white*
- *2.75mm (UK 12, US 2) metal knitting needles*

STITCHES USED
bullion, buttonhole, cable plait, chain, coral knot, couching, detached chain, double long-armed feather, feather, french knot, herringbone, long-armed feather, overcast cable plait, padded buttonhole, padded satin, palestrina, running, satin, single feather, stem, stepped buttonhole, straight, whipped buttonhole, whipped stem.

Lily 3

EMBROIDERY

❶ *Trace Pattern A (p70) onto fabric piece A. Trace Pattern B (p69) onto fabric piece B. Trace only Pattern B edging lines, large dots and stars onto the back of Piece C (p69). Use the chenille needle for all embroidery, except where otherwise indicated. Mount the fabric in a hoop so that it is drum tight.*

Piece A
Border Using the darner needle, stitch spaced french knots with 2 wraps.

Edging Work stepped buttonhole around the lower edge of the piece, starting and finishing at the large dots. Leave the edging at the top of the piece unworked.

Lily 1
Stems Work the stems for all the lilies (not just Lily 1) in coral knot stitch.

Upper left bud Work each petal section in slanting buttonhole stitch. Start at the base and work towards the tip.

Left leaves Work up each side in detached chain stitch, angling the stitches so that the chain at the tip lies along the centre vein.

Lower bud Outline the bud in coral knot stitch. Work the lines down the bud in whipped stem stitch.

Right leaves Using the darner, work alternating bullions and straight stitches up each side of the leaves. Angle the stitches so that the bullion at the leaf tip lies along the centre vein.

Forget-me-not 2
Stems Work the stems for all the forget-me-nots (not just Forget-me-not 2) in stem stitch.

Flowers Work the petals in buttonhole stitch. Work a french knot (2 wraps, darner needle) in each flower centre.

Left leaf Work the leaf in palestrina stitch, with the arms extending to its edges.

Right leaf Work as for Lily 1 Left Leaves.

Lily 3 Work the stamens and the style in couching. Using the darner needle, work a bullion for each of the six anthers, and three bullions for the stigma. Outline the petals using padded buttonhole with one layer of padding, and positioning the rolled edge as

Border and edging

Lily 1 stem and left bud

Lily 1 left leaves

Lily 1 lower bud

Lily 1 right leaves

Forget-me-not 2 stems and flowers

Forget-me-not 2 left leaf

Forget-me-not 2 right leaf

Forget-me-not 4 flowers

Forget-me-not 4 left leaf

shown in the photo. Fill each of the petals with running stitch filling.

Forget-me-not 4

Flowers Work each petal as a single detached chain stitch. Work a french knot (2 wraps, darner needle) in the centre of each flower.

Left leaf Work slanting buttonhole stitch up each side, with the rolled edges at the edges of the leaf.

Folded leaf Work the bottom half of the leaf with the outline and centre vein in stem stitch. Work the top half of the leaf in slanting satin stitch.

Right leaf Stitch the centre vein in overcast cable plait, with the overcasting extending to the leaf edges.

Forget-me-not 5

Flowers Work each petal as two detached chains side by side. Stitch a french knot (1 wrap, darner needle) in the centre of each flower.

Leaf Stitch the leaf in long-armed feather stitch, starting at the leaf tip.

Forget-me-not 4 folded leaf

Forget-me-not 4 right leaf

Forget-me-not 5 flowers

Forget-me-not 5 leaf

Lily 6 left leaf

Lily 6 lower bud

Lily 6 right leaves

Lily 6 upper bud

Lily 6 opening flower

Lily 7 opening flower

Lily 7 bud

Lily 7 left leaf

Lily 7 right leaves

Forget-me-not 8 flowers

Forget-me-not 8 left leaf

Forget-me-not 8 middle leaf

Forget-me-not 8 right leaf

Lily 9 bud

Lily 9 left leaves

Lily 9 middle leaves

Lily 6

Left leaf Starting at the base, work single feather stitch up the edge of each side of the leaf. Work the centre vein in palestrina stitch.

Lower bud Work each section in padded satin stitch (one layer of padding), angling the stitches as shown.

Right leaves Outline the leaves in palestrina stitch. From the tip, work feather stitch down the centre vein.

Upper bud Fill the outer sections with padded satin stitch (one layer of padding). With the darner needle, work spaced bullions across the centre section.

Opening flower Outline the petals in cable plait stitch. Scatter small detached chains across the centre petal.

Piece B

Border Using the darner needle, stitch spaced french knots with 2 wraps. Start level with the star on one side, work around the bottom of the piece, finishing level with the star on the other side.

Lily 7

Opening flower Work the edges of the petals in padded satin stitch, with one layer of chain stitch padding. Scatter french knots (1 wrap, darner needle) across the centre petal.

Bud Work each section in satin stitch, angling the stitches as shown.

Left leaf Outline the leaf in palestrina stitch. Fill the leaf with herringbone stitch.

Right leaves Outline the leaf in stem stitch. From the tip, fill the leaf with double long-armed feather stitch. In the gaps between the feather stitch pairs, work bullions with the darner needle.

Forget-me-not 8

Flowers Work each petal as a detached chain stitch, starting each stitch at the petal tip, and anchoring the stitches near the flower centre.

Left leaf Work each side of the leaf in satin stitch, angling the stitches as shown.

Middle leaf From the leaf tip, work long-armed feather stitch.

Right leaf From the leaf tip, work single feather stitch down each side, with the rolled edge at the centre vein.

Lily 9

Left leaves Work outlines in cable plait stitch. Starting at the tips, work long-armed feather stitch to fill the leaves.

Bud Work the outline and the lines down the bud in coral knot stitch. Work running stitch down each bud section.

PATTERN B

PATTERN C:
edging lines, large dots and stars only

Trim line

Fold line

Fold line

10

9

8

7

*Pattern shown at 50% of
full size. Photocopy the top
half and the bottom half onto
A3 pages at 200%. Match
the dotted lines and tape
them together to obtain a
full size pattern.*

Middle leaves Fill each leaf half with a layer of chain stitch padding. Work detached chain stitch over it. Angle the stitches so the one at the tip lies along the centre vein.

Right leaves Outline in spaced buttonhole stitch. Inside that, work stem stitch. From the leaf tip, fill the centre with feather stitch.

Lily 9 right leaves

Lily 9 opening flower

Opening flower Work each section in buttonhole stitch, with the rolled edge at the outer edge of each section. Whip the two centre sections of the buttonhole.

Forget-me-not 10

Flowers Work the petals in satin stitch fanning out from the flower centre. Work a french knot (2 wraps, darner needle) in the centre of each flower.

Left leaf Outline in coral knot stitch. Work the vein in whipped stem stitch.

Folded leaf From the base, work single feather stitch up each side of the leaf.

Right leaf Work as for Lily 1 Left Leaf.

Forget-me-not 10 flowers

Forget-me-not 10 left leaf

Forget-me-not 10 folded leaf

Forget-me-not 10 right leaf

Feather stitched hem

CONSTRUCTION

Trim Piece B at the trim line and discard the top section. To hem the top of Piece B, fold the fabric to the back along the first fold line. Fold it again on the second fold line to create the hem. Between the french knots on the fabric front, feather stitch through all the hem layers.

Lay right side up Piece B over right side down Piece C, matching the edges and the stars. Baste the two together, close to where the edging will be stitched.

Start at one of the large dots on Piece C. Work stepped buttonhole around the bottom of the bag, through both pieces of fabric where necessary. Finish at the dot on the other side.

Lay Piece A over the other two, and match the edges and the large dots. Stitch around the top through both pieces of fabric, using stepped buttonhole, from one large dot to the other.

KNITTED FRINGE

Using four strands of knitting cotton together, cast on 6 stitches. Using Method 3 on page 45, knit two lengths: one for the sides and bottom of the bag, and a second one to edge the entire flap section. For both, cast off 4 stitches and unravel the remaining 2.

PATTERN A

6

5

4

3

2

1

Pattern shown at 50% of full size. Photocopy the top half and the bottom half onto A3 pages at 200%. Match the dotted lines and tape them together to obtain a full size pattern.

FINISHING

When all embroidery is complete, soak to remove guide lines and wash to whiten. Press.

Neatly sew the ends of the fringe for the top flap together. Using a neat whip stitch, attach it to the edges of the top flap. Attach the other fringe to the sides and bottom, starting and finishing at the large dots. Sew the ends of the knitted part of this fringe to the knitted part of the top flap fringe where they meet.

Cut the embroidery from the surrounding fabric, taking extra care not to cut through any of the buttonhole fringe.

Blackberry table runner

This traditional-style table runner features blackberry flowers, blackberries and buds, and groupings of leaves. Two types of blackberry are used: clusters of french knots and whipped cord buttons. The button blackberries are modelled on some that were discovered on an old piece of Mountmellick embroidery.

RATING
Advanced

SIZE
42 x 84cm (16½ x 33in), excluding fringe

PATTERN
Side A of Pattern Sheet 1, Side A of Pattern Sheet 2

MATERIALS
- *50 x 92cm (20 x 36¼in) cotton satin jean*
- *No. 3 Mountmellick thread*
- *No. 22 chenille needle*
- *No. 3 darner needle*
- *3 x 50 gram balls 4ply knitting cotton, white*
- *3.25mm (UK 10, US 3) metal knitting needles*

STITCHES USED
Bullion, buttonhole, cable chain, cable plait, chain, closed feather, coral knot, cretan, detached chain, double feather, feather, french knot, indian filling, long-armed feather, overcast cable chain, overcast cable plait, padded buttonhole, padded detached chain, padded satin, palestrina knot, running, satin, seeding, single feather, stem, stepped buttonhole, trellis, whipped buttonhole, whipped cord button.

EMBROIDERY

❶ *Trace the pattern onto the fabric. The motifs are numbered on the diagram on page 73. All embroidery is worked with the chenille needle except where specified. Mount the fabric in a hoop so that it is drum tight.*

Main stems Work the main stems in cable plait stitch.

Secondary stems Use closely packed coral knot stitch.

Edging Work the edge in buttonhole stitch, angling the stitches so that they remain perpendicular to the curve.

Leaves 1 Work each half of the leaf in satin stitch, with every second stitch indented approximately 3mm (⅛in). Gradually fan the stitches so that the stitch at the tip of the leaf lies along the same line as the central vein. From the base of this stitch, work the central vein over the top of the satin stitch in cable chain stitch.

Leaves 2 Work the outline in palestrina knot stitch. Immediately inside that, work two rows of stem stitch. Fill the remaining space with lines of running stitch filling, gently curving to fit the curve of the leaf.

Blackberries 3 Work the blackberries as whipped cord buttons. Attach to the fabric with a small neat whip stitch around the edge of the buttons.

Leaves 4 Stitch the outline in closely spaced french knots (four wraps, darner needle). Work closed feather stitch down the centre of the leaves.

Leaves 5 Work the leaves in closed cretan stitch.

Flowers 6 Work the petals in padded buttonhole stitch (one layer of chain stitch padding). Work the buds in padded satin stitch (one layer of padding). Work the points on the buds as very small bullions using the darner needle. Work a ring of closely packed french knots (three wraps) around the centre section of the flowers. Work a single french knot (three wraps) in the centre.

Leaves 7 Work the border in detached chain stitch. Immediately inside this, work a line of coral knot stitch. Work palestrina stitch down the central vein, lengthening the 'arms' to fill the remaining space in the leaf.

Leaves 8 Work the outline in closely packed coral knot stitch. Immediately inside this, work a line of feather stitch. Work the central vein in coral knot stitch.

Main and secondary stems

Leaves 1   *Leaves 2*

Blackberries 3

Leaves 4   *Leaves 5*

Flowers 6

Leaves 7   *Leaves 8*

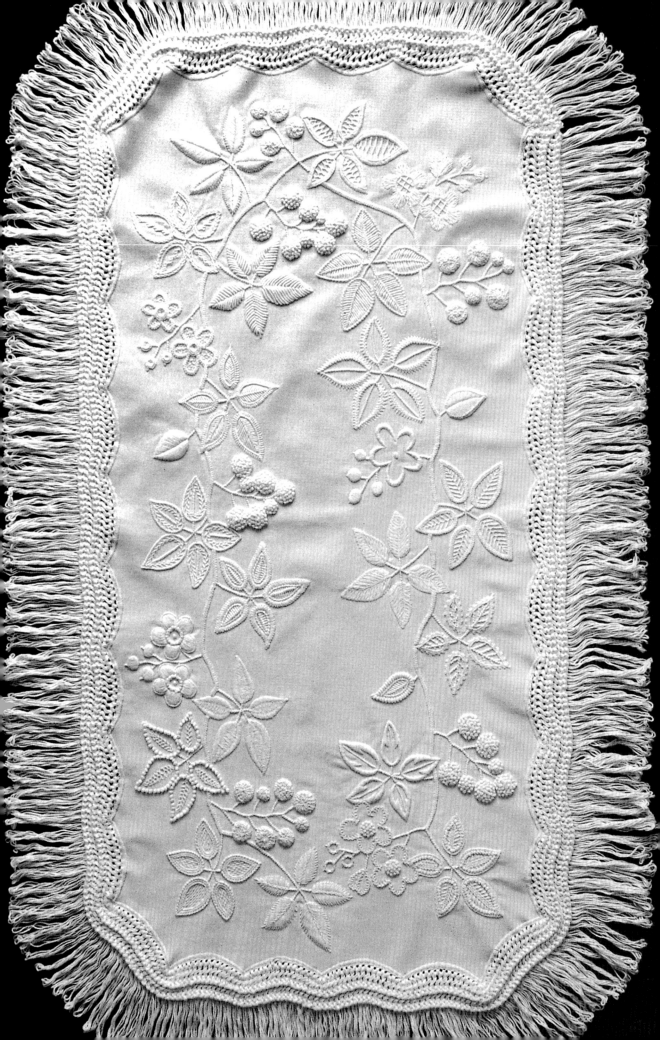

Blackberries 9 Work the blackberries in french knots. Use the darner needle and follow the diagrams (below) for stitch placement and the number of wraps of the needle required for each knot. Adjust the spacing of the knots to fill the required size.

LARGE BLACKBERRIES

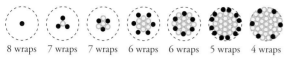

8 wraps 7 wraps 7 wraps 6 wraps 6 wraps 5 wraps 4 wraps

SMALL BLACKBERRIES

7 wraps 6 wraps 6 wraps 5 wraps 4 wraps

Leaf 10 Work each side of the leaf in padded satin stitch (two layers of chain stitch padding).

Leaves 11 With the rolled edge towards the centre, work a border of buttonhole stitch, with 1–2mm (¹/₁₆in) of space in between each stitch. Using similar spacing, work long-armed feather stitch in the centre. Leave a small gap between the buttonhole and the feather stitch.

Flowers 12 Work a border of cable plait stitch around the petal edges. In the centre of the flowers and for the buds, work rings of whipped buttonhole stitch (two rows of whipping for the flower centres, and one for the buds). Fill the petals with seeding.

Leaves 13 Using the darner needle, work bullions down each side of the leaves.

Leaves 14 Work the outline in cable chain stitch. Immediately inside this, work a line of wide stem stitch. Down the central vein, work double feather stitch.

Leaves 15 Fill the grey section of the leaf (see diagram, right) with one layer of chain stitch padding. Over the top of the padding, work 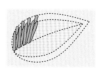 detached chain stitches, with the anchoring section of the stitch spanning the white section as shown in the diagram. Gradually angle the stitches along the leaf so the stitch at the tip lies parallel to the centre vein.

Blackberries 16 Work french knot clusters as for Blackberries 9.

Blackberries 17 Work whipped cord buttons as for Blackberries 3.

Leaves 18 Outline the leaves in buttonhole stitch, with the rolled section always on the left (see photo). This will mean the rolled section is on the perimeter of the leaf down the left side, and towards the centre of the leaf on the right side. Fill the centre with open cretan stitch.

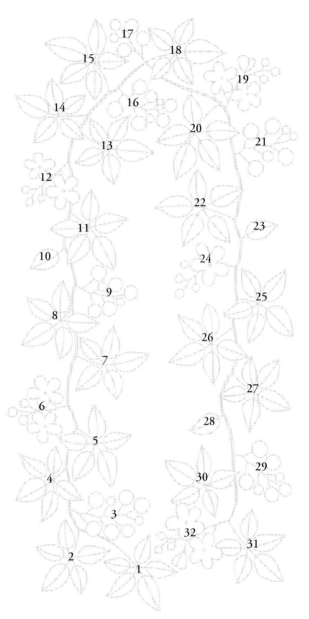

Blackberries 9

Leaf 10

Leaves 11

Flowers 12

Leaves 13   *Leaves 14*

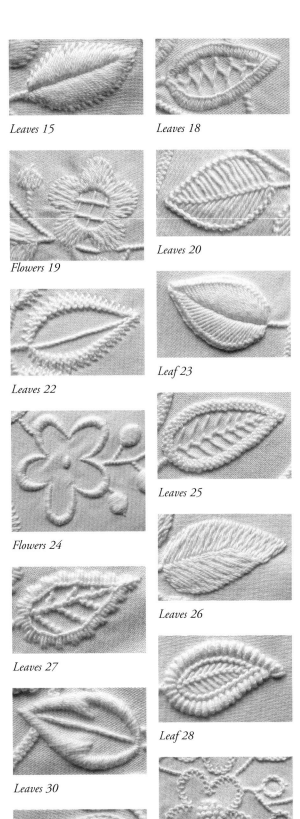

Leaves 15

Leaves 18

Flowers 19

Leaves 20

Leaves 22

Leaf 23

Flowers 24

Leaves 25

Leaves 27

Leaves 26

Leaves 30

Leaf 28

Leaves 31

Flowers 32

Flowers 19 Work the petals and buds in indian filling. Fill the flower centres with trellis, couched with half crosses.

Leaves 20 Work the outlines in palestrina knot stitch. Fill the leaves with long-armed feather stitch.

Blackberries 21 Work whipped cord buttons as for Blackberries 3.

Leaves 22 Work the outlines in cable plait stitch tapering in slightly at the top and base of the leaves. Overcast the cable plait stitch around the edge of each leaf. Work the centre veins in stem stitch.

Leaf 23 Work a single layer of chain stitch padding in each half of the leaf. Work buttonhole stitch over the padding, with the rolled section down the outer edge of each half of the leaf. Whip the buttonhole at the edges.

Flowers 24 Work the buds in padded satin stitch (one layer of chain stitch padding), with a single straight stitch for the tip of the bud. Work the outlines of the petals in padded satin stitch (one layer of chain stitch padding), tapering at the ends of the petals, and with a width of approximately 4 mm ($^1/_8$ in) at the top of the petals.

Leaves 25 Work the outlines in cable plait stitch. Fill the centres with feather stitch, extending the arms to fill the available space.

Leaves 26 Divide the leaves as shown in the diagram, and work indian filling down each half of the leaves. Angle the stitches to fit the curve of the leaves.

Leaves 27 Work the border in stepped buttonhole stitch (two up, two down), with the rolled edge towards the middle of the leaf. Work the main vein and secondary veins in coral knot stitch.

Leaf 28 Using the darner needle, work a border of alternating bullions and satin stitches. Change back to the chenille needle and just inside the border, work a line of closely spaced coral knot stitch. To fill the remainder of the leaf, work long-armed feather stitch.

Blackberries 29 Using the darner needle, work clusters of french knots, as for Blackberries 9.

Leaves 30 Work a border of padded satin stitch (one layer of chain stitch padding) in the style as shown in the diagram, right. Work the central vein in stem stitch.

Leaves 31 Work the outline in chain stitch. Inside this, work a row of closely spaced french knots (three wraps, darner needle). Reverting to the chenille needle, work the central vein in chain stitch. Fill each side of the leaf with single feather stitch, beginning at the top of the leaf.

Flowers 32 Work the petals of the flowers in cable chain stitch. Overcast the cable chain with the stitches reaching

3 mm (⅛in) inwards. Using the darner needle, work clusters of french knots in the centre of each open flower. Return to the chenille needle and work the buds in cable chain stitch. Work the point at the top of the buds as a short straight stitch.

FINISHING
When all embroidery is complete, soak to remove guide lines and wash to whiten. Press.

KNITTED FRINGE
Using three strands of knitting cotton together, cast on 12 stitches. Using Method 1 on page 43, knit a length long enough to go around the table runner. Cast off 7 stitches and unravel the remaining 5.

Neatly whip stitch the ends of the knitting together. Sew the fringe to the edge of the doily, taking small stitches through the rolled buttonhole edge and easing extra fullness into the curves. Carefully cut the embroidery from the surrounding fabric. ❦

Shamrock, thistle and rose tablecloth

This elegant circular tablecloth displays the traditional symbols
of Ireland (shamrock), Scotland (thistle) and England (rose).

RATING
Advanced

SIZE
*1.3 x 1.3m (51 x 51in),
excluding fringe*

PATTERN
Side B of Pattern Sheet 1

MATERIALS
- *1.4 x 1.4m (55 x 55in)
  cotton satin jean*
- *No.3 Mountmellick thread*
- *No.22 chenille needle*
- *No.3 darner needle*
- *6 x 50 gram balls 4ply
  knitting cotton, white*
- *3.25mm (UK 10, US 3)
  metal knitting needles*

STITCHES USED
*Buttonhole, cable chain,
cable plait, coral knot, cretan, detached buttonhole filling, detached chain, double
feather, feather, french knot,
indian filling, long-armed
feather, mountmellick, overcast cable chain, padded
satin, portuguese stem, running, stem, stepped buttonhole, trellis, whipped stem.*

PREPARATION
Find and mark the fabric's
centre by folding it in half
both ways. With a long
ruler or tape measure, from
the centre, measure 64.5
cm (25³⁄₈in) and 65cm
(25⅝in) around the entire
fabric to create two circles,
making marks with a pale
pencil or water-soluble fabric marker every 5cm (2
in). Carefully join the
marks together to make
two concentric circles
which mark the position-
ing of the buttonhole edge.

Trace the pattern onto the
fabric, matching the centre
of the fabric with the centre of the pattern.

EMBROIDERY

❶ *The motifs are numbered on the diagram, opposite. All embroidery is worked with the
chenille needle unless otherwise specified. Mount the fabric in a hoop so that it is drum tight.*

Edging Work the edge in buttonhole stitch.

Rose 1
Stems Stitch the main stem in cable plait stitch, tapering the stitching as the stem narrows. Work the secondary stems in coral knot stitch.

Rose buds Work the bud in indian filling, and the spikes
in coral knot stitch.

Opening rose Stitch the petals in indian filling. Work
the small leaves at the base in detached chain stitch.

Rose Work the petals in indian filling. Stitch a line of
whipped stem stitch along the common edges between
the petals. With the darner needle, work a ring of french
knots (three wraps) in the centre of the flower.

Leaves Work the outlines in cable plait stitch and the central veins in double feather stitch.

Shamrock 2
Stems Work the stems in stem stitch. Where the lines are
thicker, work multiple lines of stem stitch.

Rose 1 stems

Rose 1 buds

Rose 1 opening rose

Rose 1 flower

Rose 1 leaves

Leaves Work a border of stepped buttonhole stitch (one up, one down), with the rolled edge on the edge of the leaf. Fill the centre of the leaves with feather stitch.

Thistle 3

Stems Work the main stem in cable plait stitch, tapering the stitching as the stem narrows. Stitch the secondary stems in closely packed coral knot stitch.

Flowers Fill the bulb with small diamonds of satin stitch (see diagram, right). Work the outlines of the petals and bulb section in cable chain stitch.

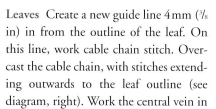

Leaves Create a new guide line 4 mm (³⁄₈ in) in from the outline of the leaf. On this line, work cable chain stitch. Overcast the cable chain, with stitches extending outwards to the leaf outline (see diagram, right). Work the central vein in

77

Shamrock 2

Thistle 3 stems

Thistle 3 flowers

Thistle 3 flowers

Rose 4 stems

Rose 4 leaves

Rose 4 opening rose

Rose 4 flower

Rose 4 buds

Thistle 6 stems and flowers

Shamrock 5

Rose 7 stems

Thistle 6 leaf

Rose 7 leaves

Rose 7 buds

cable chain stitch. Overcast on both sides so that the stitches form secondary veins.

Rose 4

Stems Use multiple lines of stem stitch for the wider parts of the stem, and single lines for the narrower parts.

Leaves Work the outline in closely packed coral knot stitch. Fill each side of the leaves with indian filling.

Opening rose Work the petal outlines in cable plait stitch. Work the small leaves at the base in satin stitch. Fill the petals with running stitch filling.

Rose Work the petal outlines in cable plait stitch. Fill the petals with running stitch filling. Using the darner needle, fill the flower centre with french knots (three wraps).

Rose buds Work the spikes in stem stitch. Fill the buds with french knots (three wraps, darner needle).

Shamrock 5

Stems Work the stems in coral knot stitch.

Leaves Stitch the leaves in padded satin stitch, with one layer of chain stitch padding. Work the satin stitch on an angle (see diagram, right).

Thistle 6

Stems Work the stems in cable chain stitch.

Leaf Work the outline in closely packed coral knot stitch. Stitch the central vein in double feather stitch.

Flowers Fill the bulb section in trellis with cross stitch couching. In each trellis division, work a french knot (three wraps, darner needle). Use stem stitch for the outlines of the petals and the bulb section. In the tip of each petal, work a french knot (three wraps, darner needle).

Rose 7

Stems Work the main stem in mountmellick stitch. Work the secondary stems in coral knot stitch.

Leaves Fill the leaves with long-armed feather stitch. With the darner needle, work a line of spaced french knots (three wraps) around the outline of the leaves.

Buds Work the spikes in stem stitch. Stitch the main part of the buds in buttonhole stitch.

Opening rose Outline the petals in buttonhole stitch, tapering the width of the buttonhole at the base of the petals. Work the small leaves at the base in detached chain stitch.

Flower Work the petals with a border of buttonhole stitch, tapering as for the opening rose's petals. Work the lines down each petal in stem stitch. Fill the centre of the flower with trellis filling with half cross couching. Work stem stitch around the outline of the centre section. Work a french knot (three wraps, darner needle) in each of the divisions of the trellis.

Shamrock 8
Stems Stitch the stems in portuguese stem stitch.

Leaves Work the leaves in closed cretan stitch.

Thistle 9
Stems Work the main stems in cable plait stitch, tapering the stitching as the stem narrows. Work the secondary stems in coral knot stitch.

Leaves Work a border of detached chain stitch, with anchoring stitches on the edge of the leaf. Immediately inside this border, work a line of stem stitch. Stitch the central vein in well-spaced coral knot stitch.

Flowers Work the bulbs in detached buttonhole filling. Outline the bulbs in cable chain stitch. Work the petals in padded satin stitch with one layer of chain stitch padding.

FINISHING
When all embroidery is complete, soak to remove guide lines and wash to whiten. Press.

KNITTED FRINGE
Using three strands of knitting cotton together, cast on 9 stitches. Using Method 2 on page 44, knit a length long enough to go around the edge of the tablecloth. Cast off 6 stitches, and unravel the remaining 3.

Stitch the ends of the knitting together. Neatly sew the fringe to the edge of the cloth, taking small whip stitches through the rolled buttonhole edge. Carefully cut the embroidery from the surrounding fabric. ❦

Rose 7 opening rose

Rose 7 buds

Shamrock 8

Thistle 9 stems

Thistle 9 flowers

Thistle 9 flowers

Clematis and fern pillow sham

This pillow sham has beautiful end designs of flowing clematis intertwined with delicate fern fronds. The centre is filled with a pattern of double bullion powdering.

RATING
Advanced
SIZE
50 x 75 cm (19¹⁄₃ x 29¹⁄₂ in),
excluding fringe
PATTERN
Side B of Pattern Sheet 1,
Side B of Pattern Sheet 2
MATERIALS
- *65 x 90 cm (25¹⁄₂ x 35¹⁄₂*
  in) cotton satin jean
- *No. 3 Mountmellick thread*
- *No. 22 chenille needle*
- *No. 3 darner needle*
- *No. 18 darner needle*
- *6 x 50 gram balls 4 ply*
  knitting cotton, white
- *3.25 mm (UK 10, US 3)*
  metal knitting needles

STITCHES USED
Bullion, buttonhole, cable
chain, cable plait, chain,
closed feather, coral knot,
cretan, detached chain,
double bullion, double
feather, double long-armed
feather, feather, french knot,
long-armed feather, overcast
cable chain, overcast cable
plait, overwrapped bullion,
padded buttonhole, padded
detached chain, padded
satin, satin, thorn.

EMBROIDERY

❶ *Trace the pattern onto the fabric. The motifs are numbered on the diagram on page 82. All embroidery is worked with the chenille needle unless otherwise specified. Mount the fabric in a hoop so that it is drum tight.*

Edging Work the edging in buttonhole stitch.

Powdering Work double bullions with the No. 18 darner.

Clematis stems and tendrils Work the stems and tendrils in coral knot stitch.

Leaf 1 With the No. 3 darner needle, work the outline as closely packed french knots (three wraps). Using the chenille needle, fill the centre with long-armed feather stitch, leaving a small gap inside the outline.

Leaf 2 Work a border of spaced buttonhole stitch, with each stitch spaced 1–2 mm (¹⁄₁₆ in) apart. Immediately inside this, work a line of coral knot stitch. Fill the centre with long-armed feather stitch.

Leaf 3 Divide the leaf as shown right. Fill the grey section with one layer of chain stitch padding. Starting at the leaf base, work satin stitch  up the sides, alternating the length of every second stitch between the inner and outer lines. Gradually angle the stitches so that the stitch at the leaf tip lies along the central vein.

Leaf 4 Work the leaf border in cable plait stitch. Stitch the main vein and secondary veins in coral knot stitch.

Edging

Powdering

Stems and tendrils

Leaf 1

Leaf 5 Using the No. 18 darner needle, work bullions up each side of the leaf, gradually angling them so that the stitch at the leaf tip lies along the central vein.

Leaf 6 Work a line of chain stitch padding just inside the edge of the leaf. Over this, work buttonhole stitch, with the rolled edge towards the centre of the leaf. Using the No. 3 darner needle, work a line of french knots (three wraps) down the centre of the leaf.

Leaf 7 Work a line of chain stitch padding just inside the edge of the leaf. Over this, work detached chain stitch, with the anchoring stitches at the edge of the leaf. Immediately inside this border, work a line of coral knot stitch. Fill the centre with feather stitch.

Flower 8 Work two layers of chain stitch padding on each petal, leaving the central sections empty. Over this, work detached chain stitch, fanning the stitches out around each petal. In the centre of the flower, work a cluster of french knots (three wraps, No. 3 darner needle).

Leaf 9 Work a border of cable chain stitch. Stitch the central vein with cable chain stitch. Work a line of feather stitch down each side of the leaf.

Leaf 10 Divide the leaf as shown. Work satin stitch up each side, between the two outer lines. Every second stitch, extend the length to the central vein.

Leaf 11 Work a border of thorn stitch around the edge of the leaf. Stitch the central vein in coral knot stitch.

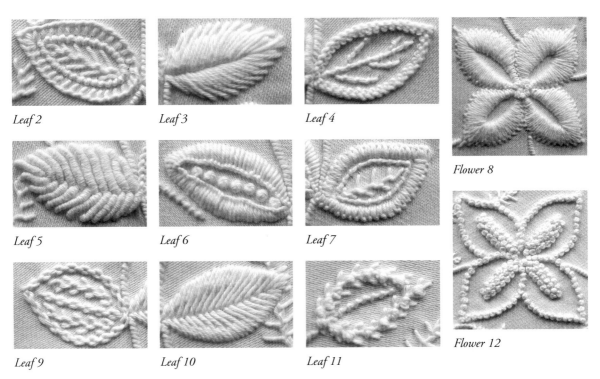

Leaf 2

Leaf 3

Leaf 4

Flower 8

Leaf 5

Leaf 6

Leaf 7

Leaf 9

Leaf 10

Leaf 11

Flower 12

Flower 12 Using the No.3 darner needle, outline the petals in french knots (three wraps). Fill each petal centre with closely packed french knots. Work padded satin stitch (one layer of padding) in the flower centre.

Leaf 13 Fill each side of the leaf with lines of buttonhole stitch as shown in the diagram, keeping the rolled section at the bottom.

Leaf 14 Fill the leaf with long-armed feather stitch.

Leaf 15 Work the outline in coral knot stitch, with knots spaced 1 mm ($\frac{1}{16}$ in) apart. Work the central vein in cable chain stitch. Overcast the cable chain stitch on both sides, so that the overcasting forms the secondary veins.

Fern 16 Work the stem in coral knot stitch. Work the side leaves in double feather stitch, with the stitching small and narrow at the top, and widening at the base of each side leaf.

Fern 17 Work the stem in cable chain stitch. Stitch the side leaves in overcast cable chain stitch, with the overcasting narrow at the top of each frond, widening at the base.

Leaf 18 Work the leaf filling as cretan stitch. Stitch the outline in coral knot stitch.

Leaf 19 Fill each side of the leaf with one layer of chain stitch padding. Over the top of this, work detached chain stitches, so that the anchoring stitches are at the edge of the leaf. Along the central vein, work cable chain stitch.

Leaf 20 Work the leaf filling in double long-armed feather stitch. Work the outline of the leaf in spaced french knots (three wraps, No.3 darner needle).

Flower 21 Work the outline of each petal in cable plait stitch. Work the centre section of each petal in wide, loosely spaced cable plait stitch. Overcast this stitching on both sides.

Leaf 22 Work an outline of spaced french knots (three wraps, No.3 darner needle). Immediately inside this, work a line of closely packed coral knot stitch. Work secondary veins down the leaf in bullion stitch, using the No.3 darner needle.

Leaf 23 Work an outline of cable chain stitch. From the top of the leaf, work thorn stitch down the central vein.

Flower 24 Work the petals in cretan stitch, fanning the stitches around the petal so that they radiate outwards. Down the centre of each petal, work overwrapped bullions across the space. Work a ring of coral knot stitch around the centre of the flower.

Leaf 13

Leaf 14

Leaf 15

Fern 16

Fern 17

Leaf 18

Leaf 19

Leaf 20

Flower 21

Leaf 22

Leaf 23

Flower 24

Flower 25

Leaf 26

Leaf 27

Leaf 28

Fern 29

Fern 30

Flower 25 Work the outlines of the petals in closely packed coral knot stitch. Work padded satin stitch in the centre of each petal with one layer of chain stitch padding. Fill the remainder of the petals with feather stitch. Using the No. 3 darner needle, stitch a cluster of french knots (three wraps) in the centre of the flower.

Leaf 26 Work a border of padded buttonhole stitch (one layer of chain stitch padding) around the leaf edge, with the rolled edge to the outside of the leaf. Work a line of closed feather stitch down the centre of the leaf.

Leaf 27 Fill each side of the leaf with padded buttonhole stitch (two layers of chain stitch padding), keeping the rolled edge to the outside of the leaf, and fanning the stitches at the tip.

Leaf 28 Work the outline in cable plait stitch, tapering the width at each end of the leaf. Work spaced french knots (three wraps, No. 3 darner needle) down the centre of the leaf.

Fern 29 Work the main stem and side leaf stems in cable chain stitch. Along the side leaves, work a detached chain stitch into each side of every second cable chain.

Fern 30 Work the stem in coral knot stitch. Work the side leaves in long-armed feather stitch, narrow at the top, widening at the base.

FINISHING
When all embroidery is complete, soak to remove guide lines and wash to whiten. Press.

KNITTED FRINGE
With three strands of knitting cotton together, cast on 9 stitches. Using Method 1 on page 43 knit a length long enough to go around the pillow sham. Cast off 6 stitches and unravel the remaining 3.

Neatly stitch the ends of the knitting together. Sew the fringe to the edge of the pillow sham, taking small whip stitches through the rolled buttonhole edge and easing extra fullness into the curves. Carefully cut the embroidery from the surrounding fabric. ❦

Projects with contemporary applications

The sturdiness and gentle beauty of Mountmellick embroidery means that it is suitable for today's decorator. These projects, while still using designs and stitches that are in the traditional style, feature more contemporary applications such as a lamp shade, framed picture, needlecase and bolster. With a little imagination, any of the Mountmellick projects in this book could be adapted to suit other soft furnishings in a modern setting.

Oak leaf needlecase

This useful needlecase introduces some of the common Mountmellick stitches.

RATING
Beginner

SIZE
8 x 12 cm (3¼ x 4¾ in)

PATTERN
Side A of Pattern Sheet 2

MATERIALS
- *40 x 20 cm (16 x 8 in) cotton satin jean*
- *No. 3 Mountmellick thread*
- *No. 22 chenille needle*
- *31 x 23 cm (12¼ x 9 in) doctor's flannel**
- *Pinking shears*

*Doctor's flannel is a fine wool flannel. The lanolin in wool prevents needles rusting.

STITCHES USED
Buttonhole, cable plait, coral knot, knotted button-hole, padded satin, seeding.

EMBROIDERY

❶ *Trace the pattern, including all guide lines, onto the centre of the fabric. Not all lines will be covered by stitching, so ensure they are removable on completion. Mount the fabric in a hoop so that it is drum tight.*

Branch Work the branch in cable plait stitch.

Leaf Stitch the outline of the leaf in cable plait stitch. Work the leaf veins and stems in coral knot stitch.

Acorn Work the acorn base in padded satin stitch (two layers of chain stitch padding). Work the acorn outline in coral knot stitch, and filling as seeding with double stitches.

Edging Work the edging in sawtooth buttonhole with a knotted buttonhole on the point of each sawtooth.

CONSTRUCTION

Cut the fabric down to 36 x 14 cm (14¼ x 5½ in), along the outermost guide lines. With wrong side facing, fold in 1 cm (⅜ in) at each end. Press.

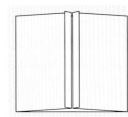

wrong side of fabric

Turn the fabric over. Fold in 8.5 cm (3⅜ in) at each end, so that the folded edges meet. Using a seam allowance of 1 cm (⅜ in), stitch across the top and base.

Clip the corners and turn right side out. Neatly whip stitch the folded edges together at the middle.

From the doctor's flannel, cut two pieces 15 x 11 cm (4⅜ x 6 in) with the pinking shears. Fold in half and mark the centre. Position the doctor's flannel pieces, one on top of the other, in the inside centre of the needlecase. Machine sew through all the layers, along the centre line, from top to bottom. Tie off ends. Fold the case and flannel in half with the embroidery facing out.

FINISHING

When all the embroidery is complete, soak to remove guides and wash to whiten. Press. ▾

Lily box

Use this pretty box which is edged in a knitted braid, to keep all your treasures in.

RATING
Beginner
SIZE
17 x 17cm (6³/₄ x 6³/₄ in)
MATERIALS
- *25 x 25cm (10 x 10in) cotton satin jean*
- *No. 3 Mountmellick thread*
- *No. 4 Mountmellick thread*
- *No. 22 chenille needle*
- *No. 3 darner needle*
- *1 x 50 gram ball 4 ply knitting cotton, white*
- *3.25mm (UK 10, US 3) metal knitting needles*
- *Papier mache box, lid 17 x 17cm (6³/₄ x 6³/₄ in)*
- *Folk art paint in colour of your choice*
- *Paint brush*
- *2 pieces polyester wadding, 17 x 17cm (6³/₄ x 6³/₄ in)*
- *Heavy cardboard, 17 x 17cm (6³/₄ x 6³/₄ in)*
- *Spray adhesive*
- *Clear, fast-drying craft glue*
- *Sewing machine thread*
STITCHES USED
Bullion, buttonhole, cable plait, chain, feather, french knot, herringbone, long-armed feather, padded satin, stem, straight, upright feather.

EMBROIDERY

❶ *Trace the pattern (p89) onto the fabric. The motifs are numbered. Use the No. 3 thread and chenille needle for all stitching, except where otherwise specified. Mount the fabric in a hoop so that it is drum tight.*

Stems Stitch the main stem in upright feather stitch, and the leaf stems in stem stitch.

Leaf 1 Working in No. 4 thread, sew rows of buttonhole stitch, stretching across the leaves so that the rolled part forms the outline and secondary veins of the leaf.

Leaf 2 Work the outline in No. 4 thread using cable plait stitch. Work the veins in french knots (four wraps, darner needle).

Leaf 3 Stitch the outline in buttonhole stitch, and the veins in feather stitch.

Leaf 4 Work the outline in tightly packed french knots (three wraps, darner needle). Fill the centre with long-armed feather stitch.

Flower

Stems

Leaf 2

Leaf 1

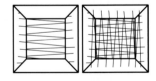

Leaf 3

Leaf 4

Flower Down one side of each petal, work the outline as bullions (use darner needle) laid side by side. Down the other side, use padded satin stitch (two layers of chain stitch padding). Work a line of herringbone stitch in the middle of each petal. Stitch the stigma in padded satin stitch (two layers of padding). At the point of the stigma, work two straight stitches in a 'v' shape.

FINISHING
When all embroidery is complete, soak to remove guide lines and wash to whiten. Press.

CONSTRUCTION
Apply spray adhesive to each piece of wadding and attach them, one on top of the other, to one side of the heavy card. Centre the embroidered piece, right side up, over this, with the wadding sandwiched between.

Fold the excess fabric around the edges of the cardboard to the back. Using double sewing machine thread, lace the fabric as shown in the diagrams: firstly from side to side, and then up and down. Tension the thread so that the embroidery stretches evenly over the front of the padded board.

Paint the inside and outside of the box and lid with two coats of folk art paint. Allow to dry. Glue the padded top to the box lid with the craft glue. Place the padded lid under some heavy books until the glue has dried.

KNITTED BRAID
Divide the ball of knitting cotton into three equal parts. Using three strands of knitting cotton together, cast on 3 stitches. Using Method 2 on page 44, knit a length of braid long enough to go around the rim of the box lid. Cast off all the stitches.

Neatly whip stitch the ends of the braid together. Using craft glue, attach the braid around the top of the lid, covering the gap between the padded top and the box lid. ❦

Pattern shown smaller than full size. Photocopy at 150% to obtain the full size pattern.

4

3

1

2

Pattern shown smaller than full size. Photocopy at 150% to obtain the full size pattern.

Framed flower spray picture

This delightful project features freshly picked forget-me-nots, daisy and fern, tied together with a bow.

RATING
Beginner
SIZE
15 x 19cm (6 x 7½in)
MATERIALS
- *30 x 35cm (12 x 14in) cotton satin jean*
- *No. 3 Mountmellick thread*
- *No. 22 chenille needle*
- *No. 3 darner needle*
STITCHES USED
Buttonhole, buttonholed feather, closed feather, coral knot, feather, french knot, long-armed feather, padded satin, stem.

EMBROIDERY

❶ *Trace the pattern (p89) onto the fabric. Work all embroidery using the chenille needle except where otherwise indicated. Mount the fabric in a hoop so that it is drum tight.*

Bow Work the outlines in stem stitch, with a line of feather stitch down the middle of each section of ribbon.

Forget-me-nots Work the stems in stem stitch. Work the flowers in buttonhole stitch. In the centre of each flower, work a french knot (three wraps, darner needle). Work the leaf in long-armed feather stitch.

Fern Work the main centre stem in stem stitch. Work the side fronds in buttonholed feather stitch, with shorter arms at the tips of the fronds, increasing gradually towards the centre stem.

Daisy flower Work the outline in closely spaced coral knot stitch. Work the filling in closed feather stitch.

Daisy stem Work the stem in padded satin stitch (one layer of chain stitch padding).

Daisy leaves Work the leaves in padded satin stitch, with

Bow and stems

Forget-me-nots

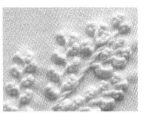

Fern

Daisy flower

Daisy leaf

one layer of chain stitch padding for the left leaf, and two layers for the right leaf.

FINISHING

When all embroidery is complete, soak to remove guide lines and wash to whiten. Press. Frame as desired. ❧

Grapes lampshade

This pretty lampshade features bunches of grapes, large leaves and twirling tendrils. This design could be adapted to fit other shades, by spacing the motifs evenly, and by repeating them if required.

RATING

Intermediate

SIZE

18 x 18 x 18cm (7 x 7 x 7 in), excluding fringe

MATERIALS

- *18 x 18 x 18cm (7 x 7 x 7in) four-sided lampshade*
- *40 x 75cm (16 x 29½in) cotton satin jean (see note)*
- *No. 4 Mountmellick thread*
- *No. 22 chenille needle*
- *No. 3 darner needle*
- *2 x 50 gram balls 4ply knitting cotton, white*
- *3.25mm (UK 10, US 3) metal knitting needles*
- *12mm (½in) bias binding, white (enough for top and bottom of lampshade)*
- *Large sheet of paper*
- *Clear, fast-drying craft glue*
- *Water-soluble fabric marker*

❶ *Use a plain white lamp shade. The existing fabric can be covered over. A different shape or size shade will require different quantities of fabric. Make a paper pattern to determine how much is needed.*

STITCHES USED

Bullion, cable chain, cable plait, coral knot, feather, french knot, satin, stem, straight.

PREPARATION FOR EMBROIDERY

Make a paper pattern of the shade by rolling the shade along a sheet of paper and marking the edges as you go. Also mark the corners of the shade if using a four-sided shade as shown here. Add 2.5cm (1in) fray/seam allowance along each edge of the pattern.

Photocopy two copies each of motifs A and B (pages 92 and 93). Cut the motifs out and position them centrally on the panels of the paper pattern, making sure that matching motifs will be opposite each other. Tape or glue in place. Trace the pattern onto the fabric, including the fray/seam allowance, the motifs and the edge of the pattern. Overcast, overlock (serge) or zigzag the raw edges to prevent fraying.

EMBROIDERY

❶ *Take care not to carry any threads across the back of the work as you embroider. These will become visible when the lamp is lit.*

❶ *Work all embroidery using the chenille needle except where otherwise indicated. Mount the fabric in a hoop so that it is drum tight.*

Motif A

Motif A This motif is worked identically both times. Work the stem in a slanting satin stitch. Stitch the outline of the leaf in cable plait stitch, and the veins in cable chain. Work the tendrils in well-spaced coral knot stitch.

Motif B Most of this motif is worked identically both times, except for the grapes, which are worked differently. Work the stem in cable chain stitch. Stitch the tendril in well-spaced coral knot stitch. Work the leaf outline in closely spaced french knots (three wraps, darner needle), and the veins in feather stitch.

Grapes version 1 Work the outlines as a ring of bullion stitch alternating with straight stitches. Work the bullions first using the darner needle, and then work a straight stitch in between each bullion. Work a french knot (three wraps, darner needle) in the centre of each grape.

Grapes version 2 Work the outer edge as a ring of cable plait stitch. Inside that, work a ring of stem stitch. In the space in the centre, work two bullions side-by-side, using the darner needle. Work the bullions so that they all lie in the same direction.

FINISHING
When all embroidery is complete, soak to remove guide lines and wash to whiten. Press.

Motif A.
Full size pattern.

KNITTING
Using two strands of knitting cotton together, cast on 6 stitches. Using Method 2 on page 44, knit a length long enough to go around the bottom of the shade. Cast off 4 stitches and unravel the remaining 2.

Once again using two strands together, cast on 3 stitches. Using Method 2 on page 44, knit a length of braid long enough to go around the top of the shade. Cast off all stitches.

MAKING UP THE SHADE COVER
With right sides together, sew the two ends of the embroidery together, using a 2.5cm (1in) seam allowance. Trim the seam allowance to 6mm (¼in) and press to one side.

Slip the shade over the existing lampshade, matching corners to corners, and pulling it downwards so that it fits snugly. Mark the edges of the shade on the fabric using pins or a

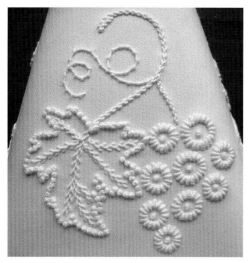

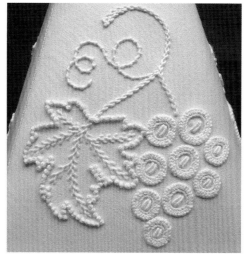

Motif B with grapes version 1   *Motif B with grapes version 2*

water-soluble fabric marker. Remove from lampshade. Adding a 6mm (¹⁄₄in) seam allowance to both ends, cut a piece of bias binding the length of the top of the shade. Open one side of the binding out. Along the other side, machine sew with a small zigzag stitch 2mm (¹⁄₁₂in) from the edge of the fold, to create the hem. With right sides together, sew the ends of the binding together and sew the opened-out edge to the top of the shade, along the line previously marked. Trim seam allowances to 6mm (¹⁄₄in). Clip the curves.

Slip the shade cover over the lampshade again. Gently pull the shade downwards to make sure that each side is taut. Pin it in place around the bottom of the shade. Mark the bottom edge of the shade on the fabric. Remove the cover from the lampshade. Repeat the binding process for the bottom edge of the shade. Wash out the water-soluble fabric marker according to the manufacturer's instructions. Gently iron the shade fabric.

Slip the cover over the lampshade. Position it once more so that it lies taut on the surface of the shade. Fold the top binding down inside the shade, stretching it around struts as necessary. Neatly glue the hemmed edge in place. Clothes pegs may be useful for holding hems in place as they dry. Repeat for the bottom edge. When the glue is dry, sew the fringe to the bottom edge of the lampshade. Sew the knitted braid to top of lampshade. ❦

Motif B.
Full size pattern.

Wildflower table runner

This contemporary table runner features flowers found growing in and around the town of Mountmellick.

RATING
Advanced

SIZE
90 x 30cm (35½ x 12in)

PATTERN
*Side A of Pattern Sheet 1,
Side A of Pattern Sheet 2*

MATERIALS
- *100 x 40cm (39½ x 16 in) cotton satin jean*
- *No.2 Mountmellick thread*
- *No.3 Mountmellick thread*
- *No.4 Mountmellick thread*
- *No.22 chenille needle*
- *No.3 darner needle*
- *Sewing machine thread, white*
- *100 x 40cm (39½ x 16 in) cotton backing fabric*
- *Heavy cardboard, 10 x 10cm (4 x 4in)*

STITCHES USED
Bullion, buttonhole, cable chain, cable plait, coral knot, couching, cretan, detached chain, double feather, french knot, herringbone, indian filling, long-armed feather, padded satin, seeding, stem, stepped buttonhole, trellis.

EMBROIDERY
❶ *Work all embroidery using the chenille needle, unless otherwise indicated. The motifs are numbered on the diagram, opposite. Mount the fabric in a hoop so that it is drum tight.*

Trace the pattern, including the seam line, onto the jean fabric. Baste along the seam line using the sewing machine thread.

Daisy 1
Stems Work in chain stitch using the No.2 thread.

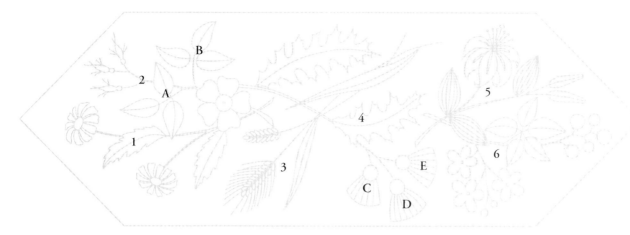

Leaves Work the border of the leaves in closely spaced french knots (three wraps, darner needle) using the No. 4 thread. Fill the leaves with long-armed feather stitch, using No. 2 thread.

Flowers Work the petals of the daisy in padded satin stitch (two layers of chain stitch padding, No. 3 thread) using No. 2 thread. Fill the centre of the daisies with seeding stitch, using No. 2 thread.

Dog rose 2

Stems Use No. 3 thread. Work the main stem in cable plait stitch. Stitch the secondary stems in closely packed coral knot stitch.

Leaves A Use No. 3 thread. Work the border and central vein in cable chain stitch. Fill the leaves with scattered french knots (three wraps, darner needle).

Leaves B Stitch in indian filling with the No. 3 thread, working each side of each leaf separately so that the inner edges of each section of indian filling form the central vein.

Buds Use No. 3 thread. Work the buds in padded satin stitch (two layers of chain stitch padding). Stitch the spikes in stem stitch.

Flower Use No. 4 thread. Stitch the border in cable plait stitch. Using the darner needle, work the stamens in bullion stitch and scatter french knots (three wraps) in the flower centre.

Wheat 3

Stems Work in stem stitch with No. 3 thread.

Leaves Use No. 3 thread. Stitch each side in detached chain stitch, anchoring the chains at the edges of the leaf.

Ears Using No. 4 thread and darner needle, work the ears in double bullions. Reverting to the chenille needle, work the spikes in couching using No. 3 thread, and couching down a single thread.

Daisy 1 leaves

Daisy 1, flower and stem

Dog rose 2 stems

Dog rose 2 leaves B

Dog rose 2 leaves A

Dog rose 2 flower

Dog rose 2 buds

Wheat 3 ear with spikes

Wheat 3 ear

Wheat 3 stems and leaves

95

Thistle 4 flower C

Thistle 4 flower D

Thistle 4 flower E

Thistle 4 leaves

Lily 5 stems

Lily 5 buds

Lily 5 leaves

Lily 5 flower

Blackberry 6 stems

Blackberry 6 flowers and buds

Thistle 4

Stem Work in cable plait stitch using No. 3 thread.

Leaves Use No. 3 thread. Work the borders of the leaves in buttonhole stitch, with the rolled edge outwards. Stitch the central vein in double feather stitch.

Flower C Use No. 2 thread. Work the thistle bulb in a diamond pattern of satin stitch. Work the petals, including the scalloped edge along the top, in satin stitch. Work a stepped buttonhole border around the bulb's lower edge, with the rolled section innermost.

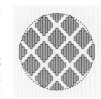

Flower D Use No. 2 thread. Work the thistle bulb in a trellis pattern, using chain stitch. Work a border around the bulb in chain stitch. Work the petal outlines in chain stitch, and scatter detached chains within each. Work the scalloped edge along the top as a line of detached chains, with the anchoring parts of the stitches outermost.

Flower E Use No. 3 thread. Work the bulb in trellis stitch, with cross stitch couching. To divide the bulb and petals, work a line of stem stitch. Around the remainder of the bulb, work a border of cable plait stitch. Work each petal outline in stem stitch. Work the scalloped edge along the top in cable plait stitch.

Lily 5

Stems Using No. 3 thread, work the stems in chain stitch, with multiple lines of stitching where the stem is thicker.

Leaves Work the outline in cable chain stitch using No. 4 thread. Work the ribs on the leaves in coral knot stitch using No. 2 thread.

Buds Use No. 4 thread. Work the outline of the buds in cable plait stitch. The line down the centre of each bud is worked in stem stitch.

Flower Use No. 4 thread. Outline the petals in cable plait stitch. Work the lines down the centre of the petals in herringbone stitch. Work the stamens and style in stem stitch. Work the anthers in padded satin stitch (one layer of chain stitch padding). For the stigma, work a double bullion at the base, with a padded satin stitch section above. Using the darner needle, fill the petals with scattered french knots (three wraps).

Blackberry 6

❶ *Use No. 3 thread throughout.*

Stem Work the main stem in cable plait stitch and secondary stems in coral knot stitch.

Flowers Work a line of chain stitch padding around the petal outlines. Over this, work satin stitch up one side of each petal, fanning the stitches at top of the petal and

96

working back down the other side. Work three french knots (three wraps, darner needle) in each flower centre.

Buds Stitch the buds in padded satin stitch, with one layer of chain stitch padding.

Leaves Work a border of closed cretan stitch around each leaf. Fill the centre with open cretan stitch.

Fruit Using the darner needle, work large and small blackberries as described on page 72. Work the small leaves at the base of each fruit in bullion stitch.

Blackberry 6 leaves

FINISHING

When all embroidery is complete, soak to remove guide lines and wash to whiten. Press.

Blackberry 6 fruit

CONSTRUCTION

With right sides together and edges matching, pin or baste the embroidered front and the backing fabric together. Stitch along the seam line basted on the embroidered front, leaving a 15cm (6in) gap on one side for turning.

Trim the seam allowance to 1cm (⅜in), and clip the corners. Turn the runner so that the right side faces out. Press. Neatly hand stitch the opening closed.

TASSELS

Use No.3 thread. Cut a 30cm (12in) length of thread and lay it across the top of the heavy card.

Wind more thread around the card 50 times (over the cut length), starting and finishing at the bottom edge of the card (this will become the bottom of the tassel). Using the cut length laid across the card, tightly tie the top of the tassel. Slide the wound thread off the card. Cut the threads at the bottom.

With a new length of thread, make a loop at the top end of the tassel, allowing the tail to hang down with the tassel skirt.

Bind a cuff around the tassel, approximately 1cm (⅜in) from the tied top. When the cuff is wide enough, slip the loose end through the loop at the top of the tassel. Pull the skirt end of the loop so that the other end of the cuff thread neatly disappears in behind the cuff, effectively tying off the cuff threads. Trim the top end, and trim the skirt end level with the bottom of the skirt.

Make a second tassel to match. Using the ties at the tops of the tassels, neatly sew them to the points at the ends of the runner. 🌱

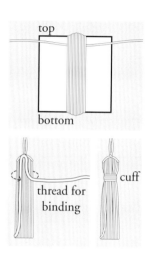

Maidenhair and passionflower bolster

This sumptuous bolster features twining passionflower and maidenhair fern.
The matt of the threads contrasts beautifully with the satin piping detail.

RATING
Intermediate

SIZE
25 x 50cm (10 x 19¾in)

MATERIALS
- *28 x 53cm (11 x 21in) cotton satin jean*
- *30cm (12in) heavy-weight white cotton fabric*
- *60cm (23½in) white cotton or polycotton (for the insert)*
- *No.2 Mountmellick thread*
- *No.3 Mountmellick thread*
- *No.4 Mountmellick thread*
- *No.22 chenille needle*
- *No.3 darner needle*
- *2.2m (86½in) white satin piping*
- *Polyester fibre fill*
- *50cm (19¾in) white zipper*
- *Sewing machine thread, white*
- *2 white tassels*
- *2 x 25mm (1in) buttons for each end of the bolster*

STITCHES USED
Bullion, buttonhole, cable chain, cable plait, chain, coral knot, detached chain, feather, fly, french knot, herringbone, long-armed feather, padded buttonhole, padded satin, palestrina knot, stem, whipped buttonhole.

EMBROIDERY

❶ *Trace the pattern (p101) onto the centre of the jean fabric. The motifs are numbered on the diagram on the next page. Work all embroidery using the chenille needle and No.3 thread, unless otherwise indicated. Mount the fabric in a hoop so that it is drum tight.*

Maidenhair fern stems Use tightly packed coral knot stitch.

Passionfruit stems Stitch the main stem using cable plait stitch. Work the small leaves near the ends of the stems using buttonhole stitch. Stitch the tendrils in stem stitch.

Maidenhair fern 1 Stitch each leaf as two fly stitches, each with its base touching the end of the stem.

Passionfruit leaf 2 Stitch the stem in palestrina knot stitch. Work a line of chain stitch padding just inside the outline of the leaf. Over the padding, work detached chain stitches, laid side-by-side, with anchoring stitches at the edge of the leaf. Using No.4 thread, down the central vein, stitch palestrina knot stitch with long arms to fill the leaf.

Passionfruit leaf 3 Work the outline and stem in palestrina knot stitch. Stitch the veins in long-armed feather stitch to fill the leaf.

Passionflower 4 Using No.2 thread, work a layer of chain stitch padding down each side of the petals. Over this, work buttonhole stitch down each side of the petals, with

Passionfruit stem and small leaves

Passionfruit tendrils

Passionfruit leaf 2

Passionfruit leaf 3

Passionfruit leaf 6

the rolled section at the edge. With No.3 thread, using the darner needle, work a ring of bullions radiating out, between the petals and the centre of the flower. In the centre of the flower, stitch a wheel of whipped buttonhole stitch, with all the whipping in one direction. Stitch the style in cable chain stitch using No.4 thread. For the stigma, work three bullions with french knots at their tips, using the darner needle and No.3 thread. Part way down the style, work five stamens in stem stitch using No.2 thread. Work a short bullion for the anthers, using No.3 thread and the darner needle.

Maidenhair fern 5 Using the darner needle, for each leaf work four bullions, fanning out from the stem.

Passionfruit leaf 6 Work the outline in cable chain stitch, using No.4 thread. Change to No.3 thread. Work the veins as well-spaced coral knot stitch. Fill the leaf with scattered french knots, using the darner needle.

Passionflower 7 Stitch the petals in padded satin stitch (one layer of chain stitch padding). With the darner needle, work bullions radiating out from the central section as for Motif 4. Fill the centre of the flower with tightly packed french knots (darner needle, No.4 thread). Work the style in No.2 and No.4 threads – use the thinner thread to couch in satin stitch over three lengths of the thicker thread. Work the stigma, stamens and anthers as for Passionflower 7.

Maidenhair fern 3 Use No.4 thread. Work each leaf using four detached chain stitches which fan out from the stem.

FINISHING
When all embroidery is complete, soak to remove guide lines and wash to whiten. Press.

CONSTRUCTION
❶ *All seam allowances are 1.5cm (½in).*

Bolster insert
To make the bolster insert, cut a piece of the white cotton or polycotton fabric 53 x 53cm (21 x 21in). Fold in half, matching the raw edges together.

Maidenhair 1

Maidenhair 5

Maidenhair 8

Passionfruit flower 4

Passionfruit flower 7

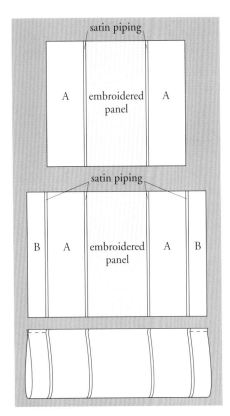

Button and tassel at bolster end

Machine sew down the edge to form a tube, leaving an opening about 15 cm (6 in) in length in the middle of the seam (this opening is for stuffing the insert with fibre fill once the ends are closed). Cut two circles 19 cm (7½ in) in diameter from the white cotton or polycotton fabric. Ease each circle into each end of the tube and, with right sides together, machine sew. Turn right side out, and stuff firmly with the polyester fibre fill. Once the insert is well filled, neatly stitch the opening closed.

Bolster cover

To make the bolster cover, cut two pieces (A) of heavy-weight cotton measuring 15.5 x 53 cm (6⅛ x 20⅞ in). Cut two pieces (B) of the same fabric, measuring 11 x 53 cm (4¾ x 20⅞ in). Also cut four lengths of satin piping, each 53 cm (20⅞ in) long.

Baste one length of satin piping down one of the long sides of the embroidered panel, matching the raw edges of the fabric and the piping. Attach a second length of binding in the same manner on the opposite side of the panel. With right sides together, take one piece A and match to one long side of the embroidered panel (with the satin piping sandwiched between the embroidered panel and piece A) and machine sew. Attach the remaining piece A to the opposite side in the same manner (see diagram, top left). Press seams towards the embroidered panel.

Baste another length of satin piping down the outer long side of one piece A. Attach the final length of piping to the remaining piece A. With right sides together, take one piece B and match to one piece A ensuring the satin piping is sandwiched between piece A and piece B, and machine sew. Attach the other piece B to the remaining piece A in the same manner (see diagram, middle left).

With right sides together, match the longest sides of the pieced cover together and machine sew the seams from each end to the first piece of satin binding, as shown in the diagram (bottom left). Baste closed the remaining gap. Press the seam open. Place the closed zipper down on the basted seam and machine sew 7 mm (¼ in) from the seam along each side. Remove the basting thread and open the zipper.

To close the ends of the bolster, machine sew a gathering thread around the raw edges of pieces B. Gather up tightly and secure. Turn bolster cover right side out. Attach one button to the centre of each of the bolster ends (to cover the gathering) and attach a tassel to each button. Ease the bolster insert inside the bolster cover and close the zipper. ❦

Pattern shown at 50% of full size. Photocopy the top and bottom halves onto A3 pages at 200%. Match the dotted lines and tape them together to obtain the full size pattern.

Appendices

APPENDIX 1 – SUPPLIERS OF MOUNTMELLICK MATERIALS

❶ *This listing is a courtesy only, and should not be regarded as a recommendation of goods or services.*

AUSTRALIA
Vetty Creations
PO Box 1723
Hornsby Westfield NSW 1635
Ph/Fax: +61 2 9477 5214
Email: yvette@vettycreations.com.au
Web: www.vettycreations.com.au

Allthreads Embroidery
122 McIlwraith Avenue
Norman Park Qld 4170
Ph: +61 7 3398 5540
Fax: + 61 7 3398 5560
Email: kerryn@allthreads.com.au
Web: www.allthreads.com.au

Josco Lace Supplies,
101 Ilford Avenue,
Arcadia Vale NSW 2283
Ph: +61 2 4975 5201
Email: joanne@joscolace.com.au
Web: www.joscolace.com.au

Sovereign Needlework
215 Mair St, Ballarat VIC 3350
Ph: +61 3 5332 1782
Fax: +61 3 5341 8367
Web: www.sovneedle.com.au

NORTH AMERICA
Berlin Embroidery Designs
1481 Hunterbrook Road NW
Calgary, Alberta T2K 4V4, Canada
Ph: +1 403 274 6293
Email: tanja@berlinembroidery.com
Web: www.berlinembroidery.com

Lacis
3163 Adeline Street,
Berkeley, California 94703,
USA
Ph: +1 510 843 7178
Fax: +1 510 843 5018
Email: staff@lacis.com
Web: lacis.com

UK AND IRELAND
Marèe Maher
157 Templeogue Road
Terenure, Dublin 6 W
Ireland
Ph: +353 01 4905132
Fax: +353 01 4515514
Email: mmaher@iol.ie

APPENDIX 2 – MUSEUM COLLECTIONS WITH MOUNTMELLICK EMBROIDERY

❶ *In many collections, the Mountmellick embroidery is not on permanent display. It is advisable to arrange any appointments with the curator well before your visit.*

An Grianán Adult Education College
Termonfechin, County Louth
Ireland
Ph: +353 41 22119,
or +353 41 22118
Fax: +353 41 22690
Email:grianan@edunet.ie
Web: www.edunet.ie/angrianan

Embroiderers Guild, Victoria
170 Wattletree Road
Malvern VIC 3144, Australia
Ph: +61 3 9509 2222
Fax: +61 3 9509 2109
Email: embgv@bigpond.net.au
Web: www.embroiderersguildvic.org

Mountmellick Development Association Museum
Irishtown, Mountmellick
County Laois, Ireland
Ph: +353 0 57 8624525
Fax: +353 0 57 8644343
Email:
info@mountmellickdevelopment.com
Web:
www.mountmellickdevelopment.com
/museum-page.html

The National Museum of Ireland
Collins Barracks, Benburb Street,
Dublin 7, Ireland
Ph: +353 1 6777444
Fax: +353 1 6777450
Email: marketing@museum.ie
Web: www.museum.ie

The Religious Society of Friends
Quaker House Historical Library,
Stocking Lane, Rathfarnham,
Dublin 16, Ireland
Ph: +353 1 495 6888
Fax: +353 1 495 6889
Email: office@quakers-in-ireland.ie
Web: www.quakers-in-ireland.org

The Ulster Folk and Transport Museum
153 Bangor Road, Cultra,
Holywood, County Down,
BT18 0EU, Northern Ireland
Ph: +44 0 2890 428 428
Fax: +44 0 2890 428 728
Email: uftm.info@magni.org.uk
Web: www.uftm.org.uk

The Victoria and Albert Museum
Cromwell Road, South Kensington,
London SW7 2RL, UK
Textiles and Fashion Department
Ph: +44 0 20 7942 2682
Email: textilesandfashion@vam.ac.uk
Web: www.vam.ac.uk

Bibliography and further reading

Balbes, Lisa M. *Mountmellick Work: The embroidery that saved a town – twice*. Needle Pointers, Vol. XXIX, Number 5 – September 2001, pages 9–13. American Needlepoint Guild, Sunwest Publishing Inc., Dallas Texas.

Beale, Edgar. *The Earth Between Them*. Wentworth Books, Sydney, 1975.

Boyle, Elizabeth. *The Irish Flowerers*. Ulster Folk Museum and Institute of Irish Studies, Queens University, Belfast, 1971.

Dawson, Barbara. *White Work Embroidery*. B. T. Batsford Ltd, London, 1987.

Enthoven, Jacqueline. *The Stitches of Creative Embroidery*. Schiffer Publishing Ltd, Atglen, Pennsylvania, 1987.

Foster, Joanna. *Mountmelllick Embroidery*. Needlework, Issue 58, July 1997, pp 38–43, Future Publishing, UK.

Houston-Almqvist, Jane. *Mountmellick Work; Irish White Embroidery*. Colin Smythe, Gerrards Cross, Buckinghamshire, 1985.

Kliot, Jules and Kaethe. *Mountmellick Embroidery*. Lacis Publications, Berkeley, California, 1998.

O'Keeffe, Regina. *The Quakers of Mountmellick*. FÁS and Mountmellick Development Association, Mountmellick, 1994.

Thomas, Mary. *Mary Thomas's Dictionary of Embroidery Stitches*. Hodder and Stoughton Ltd, London, 1934.

Townend, B. *Talks on Art Needlework*. Collins' Clear-Type Press, London and Glasgow, c1905.

Trott, Pat. *Beginners Guide to Mountmellick Embroidery*. Search Press Ltd, Kent, 2002.

Weldons Encyclopaedia of Needlework. Waverley Book Company Ltd, London, undated.

WEBSITES

http://www.vettycreations.com.au/me.html

http://islandireland.com/Pages/folk/mountmellick/embroidery.html

Index

advanced projects 71–84, 94–101
  blackberry table runner 72–75
  clematis and fern pillow sham 80–84
  passionflower and maidenhair fern bolster 98–101
  shamrock, thistle and rose tablecloth 76–79
  wildflower table runner 94–97
alternating Mountmellick stitch 33
An Grianán quilt 8
anther 15
attaching the fringe 46
back stitch 16
bag 7, 47, 60
beginner projects 48–57, 86–90
  blackberry doily 51–52
  framed flower spray picture 90
  honeysuckle doily 53–54
  leaf sampler 48–50
  lily box 87–89
  oak leaf needlecase 86
  shamrock and lily doily 55–57
blackberry 6, 10, 11
  doily 51–52
  french knot 31, 73
  table runner 71–75
  whipped cord button 39
boiling, fabric 14
bokhara couching 16–17
bolster, passionflower and maidenhair fern 98–101
botanical terms 15
box 87–89
braid stitch 24
brush and comb bag 7, 47, 60–62
bullion stitch 6, 10, 11, 15, 17–18

button, whipped cord 39
buttonhole 6, 10, 11, 12, 14
  fringe 12, 18–19
  stitch 20–22
buttonholed feather stitch 29
cable chain stitch 23
cable plait stitch 24
Carter, Johanna 7, 8
casting off 44
casting on 42
central vein 15
chain stitch 25–26
  cable chain stitch 23
chenille needles 15
clematis and fern pillow sham 80–84
coral knot stitch 26
coral stitch 30
cord button 39
cording stitch 26
cotton satin jean 6, 14
couching 27
  bokhara 16–17
  indian filling 30
  trellis filling 38
cretan stitch 27
cutting out the work 46
darners 15, 17, 31
detached buttonhole filling 10, 14, 21
detached chain stitch 26
doily 11, 12
  blackberry 51–52
  dogrose 63–65
  honeysuckle 53–54
  shamrock and lily 55–57
double bullion 11, 18
double feather stitch 28
double knot 34
double long-armed feather stitch 29
double seed stitch 16
edging 6, 11–12, 46
fabric 6, 7, 10, 14, 15
feather stitch 10, 11, 28–30

figure of eight 24
filling stitches 15
finishing a thread 15, 38
flower spray, framed
    picture 90
fly stitch 30
framed flower spray
    picture 90
french knot 6, 10, 11, 15,
    31
fringe 6, 10, 11–12
    buttonhole 18–19
    knitted 40–45
grapes lampshade 91–93
guide lines 15
herringbone stitch 10, 13
history 7–9
honeysuckle doily 53–54
indian filling 30
intermediate projects
    58–70, 91–93
    grapes lampshade
      91–93
    lily and forget-me-not
      nightdress case 66–70
    morning glory brush
      and comb bag 60–62
    oval dogrose doily
      63–65
    wheat mat 58–59
jean, cotton satin 6, 14
joining, extra yarn 41
knitted fringe 6, 10,
    11–12, 40–45
knitting cotton 11, 14, 41
knitting needles 41
knotted buttonhole 22
lace 6, 7, 12
lampshade 91–93
lazy daisy stitch 26
leaf sampler 48–50
left-handed
    knitters 41
    stitchers 15
lily and forget-me-not
    nightdress case 66–70
lily box 87–89
linear stitches 15
locked buttonhole fringe
    18–19
long-armed feather stitch
    29
loop stitch 32

McCarthy, Sister Teresa
    Margaret 7, 9
method 1, fringe 43
method 2, fringe 44
method 3, fringe 45
milliner's needles 15, 17, 31
Millner, Mrs 7, 8
morning glory brush and
    comb bag 60–62
mountmellick stitch 10, 33
needlecase 85, 86
needles 15, 17, 31, 41
nightdress case, lily and
    forget-me-not 66–70
oak leaf needlecase 86
open work 7
oval dogrose doily 63–65
overcast cable plait stitch
    24
overwrapped bullion 18
padded buttonhole 20
padded stitches 6, 10, 13
    buttonhole 20
    satin 6, 10, 11, 35
palestrina knot 34
passionflower and
    maidenhair fern
    bolster 98–101
pillow sham 7, 11, 12,
    14, 47, 80–84
portuguese stem stitch 36
potato famine 8
powdering 11
purl 45
Quakers 7
quilt, An Grianán 8
Religious Society of
    Friends 7, 8, 9
reverse chain stitch 25
runner 7, 38
    blackberry table 71–75
    wildflower table runner
      94–97
running stitch 34
sampler 48–50
satin stitch 6, 10, 11,
    34–35
sawtooth buttonhole 6, 8,
    12, 20
scalloped buttonhole 6,
    12, 21
secondary vein 15
seed stitch 16

sepal 15
shamrock 6, 11
    and lily doily 55–57
    –, thistle and rose
      tablecloth 76–79
single feather stitch 29
slip knot 42
snail trail 26
spider web 35
sprigging 11
stamen 15
starting a new thread 15,
    23, 24, 25
stem stitch 36–37
stepped buttonhole 20
stigma 15
straight stitch 37
straw needles 15, 17, 31
style 15
table runner 11
    blackberry 71–75
    wildflower 94–97
tablecloth 76–79
tendril 15
thorn stitch 11, 37
thread 6, 7, 10, 11, 12,
    14–15
    starting 15, 23, 24, 25
    finishing 15, 38
tracing 15
trellis filling 38
turning a sharp corner 20,
    23, 24, 25
up and down buttonhole
    fringe 19
upright feather stitch 30
vandyke stitch 38
washing, fabric 14
waste knot 15, 36
wavy buttonhole 21
wheat ear stitch 39
wheat mat 58–59
whip stitch 11, 39, 46
whipped 11, 15
    buttonhole 22
    cord button 39
    stem stitch 37
wildflower table runner
    94–97
worms 17
yarn 10, 15, 41
zigzagging cable chain
    stitch 23